"I WAS A BAD KID . . ."

With these words Babe Ruth starts his story. The story of a boy who was saved from poverty and perhaps worse by a God-given athletic talent. The story of a rise to fame and fortune that made him like a kid let loose in a candy store. The story of the most amazing switch in baseball history—a switch that changed one of the top pitchers in the game into its greatest slugger. The story of his sale to the New York Yankees, and the years of glory, the headline-making falls from grace, the stars he played with and against, the women he married and the one who saved him from himself, the pain of his decline, and his ultimate triumph as a human being.

It's all here—told with the fearless gusto and abiding grace of the Babe.

THE
BABE RUTH
STORY

THE
BABE RUTH
STORY

**Babe Ruth
as told to Bob Considine**

**With a New Introduction by
Lawrence S. Ritter**

A SIGNET BOOK

SIGNET
Published by the Penguin Group
Penguin Books USA Inc., 375 Hudson Street,
New York, New York 10014, U.S.A.
Penguin Books Ltd, 27 Wrights Lane,
London W8 5TZ, England
Penguin Books Australia Ltd, Ringwood,
Victoria, Australia
Penguin Books Canada Ltd, 10 Alcorn Avenue,
Toronto, Ontario, Canada M4V 3B2
Penguin Books (N.Z.) Ltd, 182–190 Wairau Road,
Auckland 10, New Zealand

Penguin Books Ltd, Registered Offices:
Harmondsworth, Middlesex, England

Published by Signet, an imprint of New American Library,
a division of Penguin Books USA Inc. Previously published in a Dutton
edition.

First Signet Printing, March, 1992
10 9 8 7 6 5 4 3 2 1

Photo Credits: The photos in this book were obtained from the following
sources: International New Photo (INP), Underwood and Underwood
(U&U), Pacific and Atlantic (P&A).

 REGISTERED TRADEMARK—MARCA REGISTRADA

PRINTED IN THE UNITED STATES OF AMERICA

This book, the only authentic story of
my life, is sincerely dedicated
to the kids of America

Contents

Introduction

Once upon a time there lived a large and muscular man named George Herman Ruth. People called him "Babe." He had a round face, a potbelly, skinny legs, and a big happy smile. Babe traveled a lot, and wherever he went, huge crowds gathered and roared their approval because he brought them joy and excitement. People said he could hit a baseball so high that it would strike a cloud and cause the rain to pour, and so far that the human eye could not follow it. It was said that his laughter could chase away darkness and make the sun shine, and that with a wink of an eye he could make a sick child well again. It has been written that he could eat twenty-five hot dogs at a sitting and then settle them with one mighty belch, and that at one time the three most famous Americans in the world were George Washington, Abraham Lincoln, and Babe Ruth.

George Herman Ruth was born on February 6, 1895, in the tough, seedy waterfront section of Baltimore, the son of a saloonkeeper. At the age of seven, his parents gave up on him and committed him to St. Mary's Industrial School for Boys, a combination reformatory and orphanage on the outskirts of Baltimore that was run by the Catholic Order of Xaverian Brothers. He was officially classified by the authorities as "incorrigible"—which, strictly speaking, means bad beyond reform, incapable of being corrected. Institutionalized at St. Mary's for most of the next twelve years, he was finally released in 1914 so he could play professional baseball.

Many people with similar backgrounds who subsequently become well known have hastily invented a more respectable upbringing. If he was anything at all, though, Ruth was genuine and unpretentious; it is doubtful if such a thought ever entered his head. He always identified publicly with St. Mary's, claimed it had been his real home, and spoke of it with warmth and fondness. In later years, he expressed his appreciation to the Xaverian Brothers by spending countless hours cheering up youngsters in hospitals and orphanages.

Ruth broke in with the Boston Red Sox only a few months after leaving St. Mary's. Harry Hooper was already a Red Sox outfielder when young George Herman Ruth first joined the team. Subsequently, he talked about what Ruth was like back then.

"People remember him," Hooper said, "with that big belly he got later on. But that wasn't there in the early days. George was 6 feet 2 inches tall and weighed 198 pounds, all of it muscle. He had a slim waist, huge biceps, no self-discipline, and not much education—not very different from a lot of other 19-year-old would-be ballplayers in those days. Except for two things: he could hit a baseball farther than anyone else, and he could eat more. Lord, he certainly did eat too much. He'd order half a dozen hot dogs, as many bottles of soda pop, stuff them in, one after the other, give a few belches, and before you knew it be ready for more."

At that time a pitcher, Ruth soon became recognized as one of the best in the major leagues. It was as a batter, though, that he began to attract even more attention. In fact, he hit so well that in 1918 the Red Sox decided to convert him into an outfielder so they could get his bat in the lineup every day instead of just one day in four.

In 1920, Boston Red Sox owner Harry Frazee sold Babe Ruth to the New York Yankees for $125,000, surely the most foolish baseball deal ever made. In 1919, his first year as a full-time outfielder, Ruth had set a new single-season home run record with 29 homers. In 1920, with the Yankees, he soared to 54 home runs; and in 1921 to 59. These would be considered remarkable home run totals even now. In those days they were astonishing. When he led the American League with 54 home runs in 1920, the runner-up had just 19. No other *team* in the league had as many home runs as Babe Ruth had all by himself. In 1921, when he led the league with 59, the runner-up had only 24.

In addition, in 1920, the Babe batted .376 and drove in 137 runs. In 1921, he hit .378 and drove in 171 runs. In all, he led the league in home runs a dozen times, in runs scored eight times, and in runs batted-in six times.

Most famous of all, of course, are his long-standing home run records—60 in a single season (1927) and 714 lifetime. The single-season record was broken after 34 years by Roger Maris, who hit 61 in 1961, and his lifetime total was eventually exceeded by Hank Aaron, who ended his illustrious career in 1976 with 755.

Nevertheless, it is still Babe Ruth, more than Roger Maris, Hank Aaron, or anyone else for that matter, who reigns as the all-time home run king. Maris hit 61 in 1961 despite unbearable pressure, but in no other year did he reach 40 and in only two other seasons did he hit as many as 30. The Babe, on the other hand, hit more than 50 home runs four times, more than 40 eleven times. And while Aaron hit 41 more lifetime home runs than Ruth, over his long career he came to bat almost 4,000 more times. At the pace Ruth hit homers (on average one every 11.8 times at bat), 4,000 more times at bat would have generated another 340 Ruthian round-trippers, for a total of 1,054!

In the 1920s and 1930s, when he was launching homers with reckless abandon, Babe Ruth became the most idolized sports figure in America, the most photographed person in the world. In the ballpark, the fans were mesmerized by his presence from the time he first stepped out of the dugout for batting or fielding practice—hours before a game was scheduled to begin—until the last out in the ninth inning. Fans in the box seats and bleachers alike, at home or away, spent most of their time watching and commenting on his every move.

During most of his career, the Babe accomplished his prodigious feats with a maximum of nightlife and a minimum of sleep. In those days there was no night baseball. With all games played in the daytime, the Babe was as free as a bird once the sun set. His first Yankee roommate, outfielder Ping Bodie, was once asked by a reporter what Ruth was really like.

"I have no idea," replied Bodie.

"What do you mean?" the reporter asked. "I thought you roomed with Babe Ruth."

"No," said Bodie, "I room with Babe Ruth's suitcase."

When the Yankees checked into a hotel, Ruth would soon be out on the town looking up old girlfriends or meeting new ones. Sometimes he'd return to the hotel briefly, and then off he'd go again. When it was time to check out, the agreeable Bodie would obligingly carry Ruth's suitcase back down to the hotel lobby.

The sportswriters loved him. To them he wasn't just Babe Ruth. He was also the "Behemoth of Bust," the "Colossus of Clout," the "Maharajah of Mash," and most of all the "Sultan of Swat." For more than a decade the *New York Daily News* had a writer (Marshall Hunt) who did practically nothing but follow

Babe Ruth around day and night. He was know⹀
Babe Ruth's shadow. The headline writers loved him
even more; aside from "Babe," their favorite name
for Ruth was "Bambino," often shortened to simply
"Bam."

"BAM HITS ONE" was a common headline of the
day.

Ruth typically batted third in the Yankees batting
order, followed by Lou Gehrig. As a result Gehrig,
one of the game's greatest hitters, rarely received the
attention he deserved.

"When Ruth's time at bat is over and it's my turn,"
Gehrig remarked once, "the fans are still buzzing
about what the Babe did, regardless of whether he
belted a home run or struck out. They wouldn't notice
if I walked up to home plate on my hands, stood on
my head, and held the bat between my toes."

Even with the mighty Gehrig batting behind him,
Ruth still received 2,056 career bases on balls, more
than any other player in history. On the other side of
the ledger, he struck out 1,330 times. (However, he
never did fan as many as 100 times in a single season,
which is commonplace today, and his lifetime total of
1,330 strikeouts is far below the all-time record of
2,597, held by Reggie Jackson.)

In terms of the social graces, Ruth was hampered
by the fact that he never remembered anyone's name.
He called all males under the age of forty "Kid" (pronounced "Keed"). Once some gray hair appeared,
they became "Doc" or "Pop." Younger women were
"Sister" and older ones, "Mom."

The ultimate in forgetfulness occurred when pitcher
Waite Hoyt was traded from the Yankees to Detroit
in 1930, after the two of them had been teammates
for a decade and close friends for most of that time.
"I hate to see you go," the Babe said, shaking hands
in the clubhouse. "Now you take care of yourself—er
. . . Walter."

Ruth had reached the end of his play-
was forty years old, more overweight
could no longer run, and his batting eye
The New York Yankees released him in
February and urged him to retire. He refused and
tried to hang on with Boston in the National League,
back in the city where his career had started twenty-
one years earlier. But he had little success, and on
June 2, with a batting average less than his weight, he
reluctantly accepted the inevitable and called it quits.

Eight days before he retired, though, he turned the
clock back—it had to be by sheer willpower—and gave
one last glorious display of Ruthian fireworks: On
May 25, at Pittsburgh's Forbes Field, he hit three
mighty home runs in one game. According to the Associated Press, the third homer (his 714th) "was a
prodigious clout off veteran Pittsburgh pitcher Guy
Bush that carried clear over the right-field grandstand,
bounded into the street, and rolled into Schenley
Park. Baseball men said it was the longest drive ever
hit at Forbes Field."

Attendance was only 10,000, but an ovation accompanied Ruth as he rounded the bases for the third
time that day—although many older fans seemed to
be crying as much as cheering. Perhaps many of them
suspected that this was an historic moment—the very
last time the great Babe Ruth would circle the bases
with his short, mincing, pigeon-toed steps in his famous home run trot.

Later, pitcher Guy Bush remembered that moment:
"He got hold of the ball and hit it clear out of the
ballpark. It was the longest cockeyed ball anybody
ever hit off me all the time I pitched in the big
leagues. That poor fellow, he could hardly hobble
along. When he rounded third base, I looked at him
and tipped my cap. He looked at me and kind of
saluted and smiled. We got in that final gesture of

good friendship. And of course that's the last home run he ever hit."

Time did not treat either Lou Gehrig or George Herman Ruth kindly. In 1939, Gehrig was diagnosed by the doctors at the Mayo Clinic as suffering from an incurable rare illness, amyotrophic lateral sclerosis, now called Lou Gehrig's disease. Within two years he was dead, not yet 38 years of age.

In the fall of 1946, Ruth started to get severe pains over his left eye. His voice also began to get hoarse. The pain became so bad that in November he entered French Hospital on West Thirtieth Street in New York City. Doctors discovered he had throat cancer, although they never told him in so many words. Surgeons operated and did what they could. When the Babe left the hospital in February, three months later, he was too frail to walk a short distance to his car without help.

Why did Ruth get throat cancer in his early fifties? It might be traced to the time in 1919 when a Red Sox trainer used an overdose of nitrate of silver in trying to cure a sore throat. More likely was Ruth's lifelong addiction to tobacco. Babe was chewing and smoking tobacco by the age of seven, and he remained a heavy smoker, especially of cigars, all his life. He also used large quantities of snuff until doctors ordered him to stop because it was damaging his nasal passages.

When he returned home from the hospital in early 1947, the Babe and journalist Bob Considine began working on this book, *The Babe Ruth Story*. With the assistance of veteran sportswriter Fred Lieb, who actually was a co-author although his name never appeared on the title page, the book was completed within the year. Coincidentally, this was the same Fred Lieb, reporting for the *New York Evening Telegram,* who in 1923 had first referred to brand-new

Yankee Stadium as "The House That Ruth Built," which is what it has been called ever since.

On June 6, 1948, in rapidly failing health, Ruth was driven to New Haven, Connecticut, where he presented the original typed manuscript of *The Babe Ruth Story* to Yale University in a ceremony before the start of a Yale-Princeton baseball game. Accepting the gift for the university was Yale captain and first baseman, George Bush.

"You know," said Ruth, "you can't put everything in a story, so I left out a few things. Maybe there should have been two books, one for kids and one for adults."

Babe Ruth died at 8:01 P.M. on August 16, 1948, in Memorial Hospital (now Memorial Sloan-Kettering) on East Sixty-eighth Street in New York City. At his bedside were his wife, Claire, his sister, Mayme, and his daughters, Dorothy and Julia. He was only fifty-three years old.

His body lay in state in a mahogany coffin placed in the main entrance of Yankee Stadium. Estimates of the number of people who filed by his bier to pay their last respects range from a hundred thousand to a quarter of a million. They stood in line for hours, all ages and social classes, many of them fathers who lifted up their small children as they passed the coffin so their offspring could say they had once seen Babe Ruth.

At the funeral, tens of thousands massed in the streets around St. Patrick's Cathedral before the requiem mass was scheduled to begin and stood silently while it was in progress. The route the funeral cortege took to the cemetery was similarly lined with unnumbered thousands who waited hours to see it pass.

Babe Ruth is buried at Gate of Heaven Cemetery in Hawthorne, New York, twenty-five miles north of Yankee Stadium.

"To really know what sort of a man Ruth was,"

sportswriter Tom Meany once said, "you have to understand that his affection for children was sincere. The Babe, for all of his lusty living, for all of his bluff and often crude ways, had ever a soft spot in his heart for kids. Every public appearance Ruth made, in his playing days or thereafter, was an inconvenience and an annoyance, but Babe never once turned down a request to go somewhere and visit kids unless it was because he had a previous obligation to visit kids somewhere else."

But it was his old friend and teammate Waite Hoyt who unwittingly uttered the most fitting epitaph of all for George Herman Ruth: "God, we liked that big son of a bitch," said Hoyt. "He was a constant source of joy."

—Lawrence S. Ritter

This Is How It Begins

I was a bad kid. I say that without pride but with a feeling that it is better to say it. Because I live with one great hope in mind: to help kids who now stand where I stood as a boy. If what I have to say here helps even one of them avoid some of my own mistakes, or take heart from such triumphs as I have had, this book will serve its purpose.

A lot of wildcat junk has been written about me in my time, along with all the flattering material that has been directed my way by two generations of sports writers. But I have often been pictured as a homeless orphan, for one thing. And it has been written that I never had much real interest in baseball, and that it never was hard work for me because the sport came naturally to me. It has even been written that I never really wanted to be named a Big League manager— because of the responsibilities that go with the job.

In the first place, I was not an orphan. Baseball was, is and always will be to me the best game in the world. I worked hard to learn it, worked even harder to keep playing it after I should have retired. As for the report that I never wanted to be a manager, that's nutty.

My mother, whose maiden name was Schanberg, lived until I was 13. My father, George Herman Ruth, lived until my second year in the majors. Few fathers and sons ever looked more alike than my Pop and I. My mother was mainly Irish, and was called Kate. My father was of German extraction. It is not true that our family name was Erhardt, as has been repeatedly written. Or Ehrhardt, or Gearhardt.

I hardly knew my parents.

I don't want to make any excuses, or place the blame for my shortcomings as a kid completely on persons or places. I might have been hard to handle if I had been born J. Pierpont Morgan V.

Yet I probably was a victim of circumstances. I spent most of the first seven years of my life living over my father's saloon at 426 West Camden Street in Baltimore. When I wasn't living over it, I was living in it, studying the rough talk of the longshoremen, merchant sailors, roustabouts and water-front bums. When I wasn't living in it, I was living in the neighborhood streets. I had a rotten start and it took me a long time to get my bearings.

My older brother, John, died before he could be of any help to me. My sister, Mayme, who still lives in Baltimore, never had much control over me. My father and mother, trying to eke out a living for all of us, worked 20 hours a day trying to make a go of the barroom. Whatever I did to bother them was amplified a hundred times by the other cares they had in life.

On June 13, 1902, when I was seven years old, my mother and father placed me in St. Mary's Industrial School in Baltimore. It has since been called an orphanage and a reform school. It was, in fact, a training school for orphans, incorrigibles, delinquents, boys whose homes had been broken by divorce, runaways picked up on the streets of Baltimore, and children of poor parents who had no other means of providing an education for them.

I was listed as an incorrigible, and I guess I was. Looking back on my early boyhood, I honestly don't remember being aware of the difference between right and wrong. If my parents had something that I wanted very badly, I took it, but I must have had some dim realization that this was stealing because it never occurred to me to take the property of anyone besides my immediate family. I chewed tobacco when I was seven, not that I enjoyed it especially but—from my observations around the saloon—it seemed the normal thing to do.

I was released from St. Mary's in July, 1902, but my parents returned me there in November of the same year. My people moved to a new neighborhood just before Christmas, 1902, and I was released to them again. This time I stayed "out" until 1904, but then they put me back again and I was not released again until 1908. Shortly after my mother died I was returned to St. Mary's once more by my father. He took me back home in 1911 and returned me in 1912. I stayed in the school—learning to be a tailor and shirtmaker—until February 27, 1914. The last item in my "record" at St. Mary's is a single sentence, written in the flowing hand of one of the teachers. It read:

"He is going to join the Balt. Baseball Team."

I believe it is customary for a man whose education was acquired as mine was to look back on those days either with scorn or a wish to conceal the facts. I look back on St. Mary's as one of the most constructive periods of my life. I'm as proud of it as any Harvard man is proud of his school, and, to get crude for a moment, I will be happy to bop anybody on the beezer who speaks ill of it.

It was at St. Mary's that I met and learned to love the greatest man I've ever known. His name was Matthias—Brother Matthias of the Xaverian Order, a Catholic order which concentrates on work among underprivileged boys here and in Europe. The headquarters of the Order are in Belgium.

I saw some real he-men in my 22 years in organized baseball and in the years since my retirement in 1935. But I never saw one who equalled Brother Matthias.

He stood six feet six and weighed about 250. It was all muscle. He seldom raised his voice, a sharp contrast to what I had known at home and in my neighborhood. But when he spoke he meant business. One afternoon at St. Mary's some of the older boys, real hoodlums, started a roughhouse in the yard and for a time it looked like they'd take charge of everything weaker than they were. Brother Matthias was sent for. He was up the road at Mt. St. Joseph's, a fancier place also run by the Xaverians. He leaped in his carriage, laid a whip on the old plug that pulled it and drove very fast to St. Mary's. Then he stood on a piece of high ground in the yard, and just looked out over the uprising. A great silence came over the yard, and the trouble stopped immediately.

He was that kind of fellow.

It wasn't that we were afraid of Brother Matthias. Some men just have an ability to command respect, and love, and Brother Matthias was one of these. He could have been anything he wanted to be in life, for he was good-looking, talented and dynamic. Yet he had taken vows of chastity and poverty and shut himself off from the world.

I don't know why, but he singled me out when I first came to St. Mary's. It wasn't that I was his "pet." But he concentrated on me, probably because I needed it. He studied what few gifts I had and drew these out of me and amplified them. He always built me.

Brother Matthias saw very early that I had some talent for catching and throwing a baseball. He used to back me into a corner of the big yard at St. Mary's and bunt a ball to me by the hour, correcting the mistakes I made with my hands and feet. When I was eight or nine I was playing with the 12-year-old team. When I was 12 I was with the 16-year-olds, and when I was 16 I played with the best of the many teams we had in school. All because of Brother Matthias.

I think I was born as a hitter the first day I ever saw him hit a baseball. I can remember it as if it were yesterday. It was during the summer of 1902, my first year in St. Mary's. The baseball of that time was a lump of mush, and by the time St. Mary's got hold of one it was considerably less.

But Brother Matthias would stand at the end of the yard, a finger mitt on his left hand and a bat in his right, toss the ball up with his left hand and give it a terrific belt with the bat he held in his right hand. When he felt like it he could hit it a little harder and make the ball clear the fence in center field. The ball would have to carry at least 350 feet, a terrific knock in those days and a real sock—in view of the fact that it was hit with one hand—even today when the ball makers are crowding the whole rabbit into each ball.

I would just stand there and watch him, bug-eyed. I had never seen anything like that in my life, nor anyone who was even close to Brother Matthias when it came to manliness, kindness and grace. He became my ideal and I tried, in my feeble way, to do things as he did them. I even learned to walk as he did—with a toeing-in manner which I still have.

Brother Matthias never lost patience with me, no matter what I did. I think he missed me whenever I'd leave St. Mary's, but he'd make a little ceremony out of each "parole." He'd tell me that I was on my way, that I'd make a go of things and become a hard-working and industrious part of the community. We'd shake hands and I would head back for the waterfront. It was the only place I knew. But, presently, I'd be back again and though I guess he was disappointed he never let me know he was. He made me welcome—and there was always a place for me on one of his teams. When I'd have trouble with my studies, or my tailoring work, he'd help me—though he had a hundred other things to do. He taught me to read and write—and he taught me the difference between right and wrong.

It was Brother Matthias who made me a pitcher. He did it to take me down a notch. I played a lot of baseball at St. Mary's but I never had any hope of making a career of the game, and I guess I never would have played it professionally if Brother Matthias hadn't put me in my place one day and changed not only my position on the field but the course of my life.

You see, I thought of myself as a pretty good catcher. Brother Matthias and others at the school tried to explain to me that left-handed catchers just do not make sense. But it was the position I liked best and the only one I claimed I could play with any skill. We had no catcher's mitt built for left-handers, of course. We were lucky to have any kind of mitt. I'd use the regular catcher's mitt on my left hand, receive the throw from the pitcher, take off the glove and throw it back to him left-handed. When I had to throw to a base, trying to catch a runner, I'd toss the glove away, grab the ball with my left hand and heave it with everything I had.

Occasionally Brother Matthias would move me around to various positions, infield and outfield. But the first time he put me in the box to pitch came when I displeased him. He put me in to show me up. I was 14 or 15 and we were playing a game in which we were taking a terrific beating. One pitcher after another was being knocked out of the box and finally it seemed funny to me. When our last pitcher began to be hit all over the lot I burst out laughing at him. I guess I said a few things too.

Brother Matthias called time immediately and walked over to the catcher's box.

"What are you laughing at, George?" he asked me in his strong but gentle way.

"That guy out there—getting his brains knocked out" I howled, doubled over with laughter.

Brother Matthias looked at me for a long time.

"All right, George, *you* pitch," he said.

I stopped laughing.

"I never pitched in my life," I said. "I can't pitch."

"Oh, you must know a lot about it," he said casually. "You know enough to know that your friend isn't any good. So go ahead out there and show us how it's done."

I knew he meant business. I put aside my mask and catcher's mitt, borrowed a finger mitt and walked out to the mound. I didn't even know how to stand on the rubber, or how to throw a curve or even how to get the ball over the plate.

Yet, as I took the position, I felt a strange relationship between myself and that pitcher's mound. I felt, somehow, as if I had been born out there and that this was a kind of home for me. It seemed to be the most natural thing in the world to start pitching—and to start striking out batters. I even tried a curve or two, and, kidlike, curled my tongue to the corner of my mouth while doing it. It became a habit that I carried into the Major Leagues with me, and I couldn't break it until Bill Carrigan, my first Big League manager, convinced me that I was "telegraphing" every curve with my tongue.

Brother Matthias saw to it that I didn't get far away from the pitcher's box during my last two seasons at St. Mary's. But he knew there was a time for play and a time for work. I could never duck a class to get to the ball field, never pass up any of the work I had to do in the tailor shop. Tailoring was to be my trade, the trade that would take me away from the waterfront when, at 21, I would leave St. Mary's and try to make my way in the world.

But baseball won out. Through baseball, I got the second break of my life. The first break, it will always seem to me, was the fact that I met Brother Matthias. He was the father I needed.

In this great land today baseball is providing breaks for other youngsters, some of them as hard and unknown as I was. It is a great calling for a boy, but it is only one of countless fields which an American boy can enter and try his hand at.

Too many youngsters today believe that the age of opportunity has passed. They think it ended about the time people stopped reading Horatio Alger.

There are more opportunities today than when I was a boy. And all of these opportunities are open to every type of American. The greatest thing about this country is the wonderful fact that it doesn't matter which side of the tracks you were born on, or whether you're homeless or homely or friendless. The chance is still there. I know.

There are half a dozen stories about my "discovery." Perhaps several of them are true, for events took place which seemed to have no connection with me and therefore went unnoticed by me.

Roger Pippen, an old friend and playing mate who is sports editor of the Baltimore *News-Post*, insists that Jack Dunn, boss of the Baltimore Orioles, and my first boss in organized baseball, signed me without ever seeing me play. Dunn told Pippen in later years that he had made up his mind about me early in 1914 when, during a visit to St. Mary's, he saw me skating on a frozen path in the yard.

Dunnie is supposed to have said, "I can tell from the way that kid handles himself that he's a natural athlete." Perhaps he did see me sliding about the yard. I sure did it often enough, when the ice was right. But, if that was so, it made no more impression on me than any casual bystander would make on any other kid concentrating on a bit of fun.

There is another story, told by some of the Xaverian Brothers, that Brother Gilbert, my late old friend and adviser who at that time was teaching at Mt. St. Joseph's, tried to lift me out of St. Mary's to help his ball club at the Mount get past a tough series. When Brother Paul, superintendent at St. Mary's, refused to let me pitch for the swank school up the road, Brother Gilbert became mad as a hornet and told his friend Paul that, just for that, he'd persuade Jack Dunn to sign me up and remove me not only from St. Mary's "varsity" ball club, but from the school itself.

That doesn't sound much like Brother Gilbert but, as I say, it is a story that Xaverians still tell.

The other story which probably has some truth in it is that Brother Gilbert had promised Jack Dunn to turn over a player to him for the 1914 season, and Dunn, holding him to his promise, asked for a boy named Ford Meadows.

Meadows was all for accepting, but Brother Gilbert wanted him to finish his schoolwork at the Mount, and, I guess, also wanted his services that season with the Mount team. Dunn was disappointed but Brother Gilbert remembered me, urged Dunn to look at me and brought him down to St. Mary's.

Whatever the preliminaries, my first knowledge that I was going to be a professional ballplayer instead of a tailor came in the middle of February, 1914. I was throwing a baseball around the still-frozen yard at St. Mary's—dressed in tight-fitting overalls, by the way—when Brother Gilbert, Dunn, Brother Matthias and Brother Paul appeared. Brother Gilbert introduced Dunn to me.

Dunn had "heard about me," he said and, to my complete surprise, asked me if I'd like to sign with the Orioles. To me, it was as if somebody had suddenly popped up and asked me to join the U. S. Senate.

I looked up at Brother Matthias' face, for explanation, and he turned to his superior, Brother Paul. Brother Paul spoke to Dunn.

"George is supposed to stay here at St. Mary's until he's 21," Brother Paul explained. "We would all be happy to see him given an opportunity to prove himself in baseball, but there are certain legal difficulties. You would have to become his legal guardian, and be responsible for him."

Dunn looked me over and said he'd take a chance. Then he said, "Now, about his salary——"

I guess my jaw must have dropped.

"You mean you'd pay me?" I gasped. My voice cracked and he laughed.

"Sure, George. I'll start you out at six hundred a year."

It made me as lightheaded as if I had been hit on the head with a bat.

"You mean six hundred *dollars?*" I asked him, unable to believe that I was the one they were talking about.

"That's right," Dunn said. "And if you're as good as Brother Gilbert and the others say you are, you'll be earning more than that in a short time."

I had some great moments in the years that followed that, including the day I signed a contract for $80,000 a year with the New York Yankees. But none of my later thrills ever topped the one I got that cold afternoon at St. Mary's when $600 seemed to me to be all the wealth in the world.

Dunn seemed content to wait until he took me to the Orioles spring training camp at Fayetteville, N. C., before he took a good look at me. He signed the papers which made him accountable to a Maryland court for my welfare and on February 27, 1914, he came to the barred gate at St. Mary's to claim me. What few clothes I had had been packed for days and I had said good-by dozens of times to every boy I knew in the school. Now I said good-by to Brother Matthias, Brother Paul and Brother Albert, who was our sports supervisor. The barred gate was unbolted and I walked out to join Dunn.

I was 19 and the proudest, greenest kid in the country. I stood a little over six feet tall and weighed less than 160. I could chew nails.

I'll never forget the ride to the railroad station, the day I left Baltimore. The whole thing still seemed like a dream to me. There were moments when I felt I sat on the top of the world, and moments when my stomach turned over—wondering if I could make the grade and fearful that I'd fail, and be forced to come back to St. Mary's. And that wasn't because I didn't like St. Mary's. I just couldn't have stood the shame of coming back, after saying good-by and after hearing Brother Matthias tell me, in his quiet way, "You'll make it, George."

There were other players on the railroad platform—players who knew each other well, and talked and moved with great confidence. Few of them paid any attention to me. But that didn't matter. The important thing was that I was going with them to spring training camp, and going on a *train*. It was my first trip out of Baltimore—my first ride on a train.

I couldn't sleep that night, wondering what it would be like in the morning and all the days and months after that. There was another reason I couldn't sleep. One of the older players, a catcher named Ben Egan, had easily talked me into the oldest gag in baseball. He told me, as dumb rookies before and after me have been told, that the little clothes hammock that reached from one end of my berth to the other was put there in order for me to rest my pitching arm. I held the arm up in this uncomfortable position all night, because I wanted to act like a pro. I wanted to be a complete part of this still unbelievable break that had freed me from St. Mary's two years before my final release time and had brought me the promise of wealth and fame.

The train pulled into Fayetteville early the next morning with the first Oriole injury of the 1914 season. A rookie named Ruth had a cramped and sore pitching arm, thanks to the "rest" he had carefully given it.

2

Babe in the Sticks

I haven't got the best memory in the world, but it is easy to recall those early days at my first spring training camp.

I got to some bigger places than Fayetteville after that, but darn few as exciting. It was the place where Jim Thorpe, one of my sports heroes, had played a little pro baseball during his summer vacations from Carlisle. Somebody blew the whistle on him, after Jim had become a world hero in the 1912 Olympics and he was forced to give back all the medals and trophies he won in that amateur competition.

Thorpe had left quite a rep in Fayetteville. Some of the town loafers used to get him full of firewater now and then and bet him he couldn't break this or that object with his head—using his head as a kind of battering ram as he sometimes did on the football field.

One night they talked him into charging a plate-glass show window. Jim took the bet, got a running start from the street, streaked across the pavement head down and splintered the big window into a thousand pieces. He won the bet, but a big chunk of the glass nearly scalped him which was a kind of interesting twist at that, considering what some of his forebears used to do to some of the early Americans who were stealing the Indians' lands.

But maybe Jim had a good time in Fayetteville. I know I did from the morning I got there in 1914 accompanied by my hammock-sore arm. For days I couldn't get over the fact that it was warmer in Fayetteville than in Baltimore, and I began to think that I should have paid more attention to geography at St. Mary's.

It still made me dizzy to think about making $600 for that season. True, there wouldn't be any money coming to me, in $100-a-month payments, until after the regular 1914 International League season began. But I was like a guy who has just been told he's the chief beneficiary of a new will that his 100-year-old rich uncle has just made. The money was as good as mine.

That wasn't all. Jack Dunn took me aside, just before we got to Fayetteville, and slipped me five dollars in advance, and it was more money than I had ever had in my pocket before.

But miracles kept happening. We went to our hotel for breakfast and while I was studying the menu I heard a player near me say, "Order anything you want, Kid. The club pays our feed bills during spring training."

I looked at him, unable to believe it.

"You mean I can eat anything I want, and it won't cost me anything?" I asked him.

"Sure. Anything."

I was on my third stack of wheatcakes and third order of ham, and hadn't even come up for air, when I realized that some of the other fellows were watching me. I looked at them silently, and kept chewing.

"I wouldn't have believed it if I hadn't seen it," Roger Pippen, one of the Orioles, said.

I grinned at him. "A guy's got to be strong to play ball," I said.

Dunn dropped by my table and took a look at the ruins. He smiled at me and put his hand on my shoulder. "We've got 27 other fellows on this club, George," he said. "Leave them a little food, will you?"

I got the name Babe during those first few days in Fayetteville. It came out of a couple of incidents. Even in those days Dunn already had a reputation for picking up very young players and developing them. Some of his older players used to kid him a lot about the baby-faced kids he concentrated on, and the first time they saw me with him—on the field—was no exception.

On that day, Dunn practically led me by the hand from the dressing room to the pitcher's box. I was as proud of my Orioles' uniform as I had been of my first long pants. Maybe I showed that pride in my face and the way I walked.

"Look at Dunnie and his new babe," one of the older players yelled.

That started it, I guess. But the clincher came a few days later. It had gotten to be a joke, the way I walked around wide-eyed all the time. I used to get up at five in the morning and walk down to the station to see the trains go through, but I always got back to the hotel in time to be first in line for the opening of the dining room.

The hotel elevator was just about the greatest piece of mechanism I had ever seen up to that point in my life. I'd ride up and down on it by the hour, just for the ride and to watch how the Negro operator worked it and how close he'd come to getting the thing on a level with the floor stops. Finally, one day, I couldn't keep my hands off the control another minute. I gave the operator most of the money I had left from what Dunnie had given me and bribed him to let me handle it myself.

My playing life, in fact my life, nearly ended a few minutes later. I left a door open on the third floor and was rubbernecking up and down the corridor while I made the elevator go up another flight. Suddenly a player screamed at me to pull my fool head inside, and I did—just in time to keep it from being crushed.

Dunnie bawled me out until the stuffings ran out of me, and what he didn't say to me the older players said for him. But finally one of them took pity on me, shook his head and said:

"You're just a babe in the woods."

After that they called me Babe.

Pippen, who was made my roommate, and whose name I just couldn't remember as long as I roomed with him, helped tone me down and get me ready for my first game as a pro. And as things turned out, Roger drove out a double which scored me in the early innings with the first run of my 22 years in organized baseball.

We had a better system of spring training in 1914 than we have today. We took our time getting ready to play, and by stepping up our work a little each day we got our rusty muscles accustomed to the strains and knocks and just about eliminated sore arms and charley horses, the standard troubles of modern ballplayers. Today a player who hasn't gone in for a lick of exercise through the whole winter and spring arrives at training camp just in time to be tossed into a regulation exhibition game that has been arranged—months before—to help pay the cost of spring training. That system and, of course, night ball, is taking years off the playing lives of thousands of modern ballplayers.

At Fayetteville, Dunnie saw to it that we took things easy for a long time, and when we did finally have a game it was one of those intra-squad games. Dunnie picked the teams and named one side the Sparrows and the other the Buzzards. I played shortstop for the Buzzards for half the game, then finished in the box.

Late in that game I hit the first professional home run of my life. I hit it as I hit all the others, by taking a good gander at the pitch as it came up to the plate,

twisting my body into a backswing and then hitting it
as hard as I could swing.

The ball cleared the right-field fence and landed in
a cornfield beyond. I don't have to tell you what it
did to me, inside, but the effect on Dunnie and the
others was easy to see, too. They estimated that it had
carried about 350 feet. I guess that doesn't sound like
much in these days of the stitched golf ball, but they
said it was pretty sensational for me because I was,
first of all, a pitcher, and next, a raw rookie.

And this was long before anybody heard of the
lively ball, when a guy like Frank Baker could win the
title of "Home Run Baker" with eight to 12 home
runs a season.

Here's the box score of my first professional game:

BUZZARDS   SPARROWS

	Ab.	R.	H.	O.	A.			Ab.	R.	H.	O.	A.
Hurney, c.	3	2	1	2	2		Potts, c.	4	2	2	3	2
Jarm'n p. ss.	4	2	1	0	0		Cr'ton, p. cf.	2	2	0	0	3
Egan, 1b.	4	2	2	12	0		Stein'n, 1b.	3	1	1	12	1
Cottrell, 2b.	4	3	3	2	3		Danf'th, 2b.	2	1	0	2	2
Ruth, ss. p.	3	2	2	1	2		Lidgate, ss.	2	0	0	0	1
Russell, 3b.	4	0	1	2	1		Lamotte, 3b.	3	2	1	4	0
Klin'h'r, lf.	2	0	1	1	0		Caporel, lf.	3	1	1	0	0
Pippen, cf.	3	2	2	0	1		McK'y cf. p.	3	0	1	0	1
Masn'a p. rf.	3	2	1	1	0		Morri'ste, rf.	3	0	1	0	0
Totals	30	15	14	21	9		Totals	25	9	7	21	10

Buzzards	1	7	4	0	0	0	3—15
Sparrows	1	0	1	1	5	0	1—9

Errors—Hurney, Steinmann, Danforth. Two-base hits—Egan, Morrisette,
Pippen, Cottrell. Three-base hit—Pippen. Home run—Ruth. Stolen bases—
Lidgate, Pippen. Left on bases—Buzzards, 6; Sparrows, 7. Base on balls—
Off Jarman, 3; Cranston, 3; McKinley, 1. Hit by pitcher—By Cranston
(Klingelhoefer). Struck out—By Jarman, 2; Cranston, 2; Ruth 1. Wild
pitches—Jarman, Cranston. Umpire—Fewster. Time, 1.45.

Courtesy Baltimore *News-Post* and Roger Pippen.

I pitched against Baker that spring and never knew
it. His team, the Athletics, were then the World's
Champions, having beaten the Giants the year before.

But that didn't mean anything to me. At St. Mary's we were too busy to read papers, or, if we did, to catch the significance of the sports pages. I was just beginning to find out there were two major leagues, the American and the National. I don't remember whether the Athletics trained at Wilmington, N. C., but, anyway, we played the A's there and I beat them. They told me I struck out Baker a couple of times and that Eddie Collins didn't get a foul off me. But I didn't know who they were. I just threw my fast one up at Mack's players with all I could put in back of it.

But Jack Dunn was a very smart baseball man and already had tried to teach me that a pitcher had to know more than how to throw them past the hitters. Even as a wild kid I realized Jack knew a lot about baseball and wanted to help me win. There was a coach named Steinman with us and Dunn told him to keep his eye on me. Ben Egan, our catcher, who had been with the Athletics, also was one of the first players I went around with.

Egan was my special friend. In those days old players paid little attention to rookies; in fact, they made it as tough as they could for them. They resented improvement in rookies. It makes me laugh how easy some of the kids have it today when they break in— what with coaches, scouts and older players all trying to instruct them. In my day you'd get a swift kick sooner than you'd get a word of encouragement. A pitcher would have to fight for a chance to take batting practice. But even if Egan played jokes and tricks on me he took my part if other players went too far, and as he did most of my catching he gave me my first signs and a lot of good pointers.

We had a funny season in Baltimore in 1914. That year the Federal League came into town and they put up a field right across from Dunn's park. It was backed by Ned Hanlon, the manager of the famous old Baltimore Orioles of the National League. Mickey

Doolan and Otto Knabe, the Phillies' infield pair, Jack Quinn, who later became my teammate on the Yankees, "Kaiser" Wilhelm, Harry Swacina and Johnny Bates were some of the players who jumped to the Baltimore Federals from the majors.

Dunn tried to fight the Baltimore Federals by putting together one of the best teams that ever has represented a Minor League club. I know our 1914 players could have beaten many second-division clubs I have seen since in the majors. We had players like Birdie Cree and Bert Daniels, former Yankee outfielders; Fred Parent, former crack Red Sox shortstop; Claude Derrick, former Athletic infielder; Neal Ball, the guy who made the majors' second unassisted triple play in Cleveland; Egan, Ernie Shore and some other good ones.

Even though I started at only $600, Dunn had a big Minor League pay roll for those days. The Federal League had hiked up salaries all along the line. We started to win early, and soon were far in front. But the town turned its back on us. Baltimore had had National and American League teams in the past and it swallowed the Federal League team hook, line and sinker. The Baltimore Feds would play to 20,000 and we'd play to 20. I am not kidding. Once when we were as far in front as the Yankees used to be in the American League we played to only 17 people. I was a Baltimore kid, winning almost every time I pitched, and hitting .300, but they wouldn't come out to see me. For I was on the Minor League team.

I still have the box score of my first International League game, played in Baltimore on April 22, 1914. We met the Buffalo club and I shut them out with six hits, the Orioles winning, 6 to 0. Big George McConnell pitched for Buffalo and we got to him early for three runs in both the first and third innings. I got two of our 10 hits but they both were singles. I walked four and struck out four. One of the reasons why this game sticks in my mind is that Joe McCarthy, who later managed the Yankees for many years, was the Buffalo second baseman, and Paul Kritchell, who scouted for the Yankees during my 15 years with them, was the catcher for the Bisons.

After the game was over Dunnie slapped me on the back and said, "Nice going, kid! Keep pitching like that and no one can stop you from getting into the big leagues."

I went out and celebrated, just as soon as I got my first paycheck—$100. I bought a bicycle, something that I had wanted and often prayed for through most of my young life. Most of the Orioles, of course, had cars, but none of them was as proud as I was, riding the first possession of my life through the old streets of Baltimore.

I got to the big leagues sooner than anybody expected.

About midseason of 1914 Dunnie saw that he couldn't cope with the competition and began to get rid of his stars to Major League clubs for the best prices they would bring. I knew a lot of clubs were after me after I had beaten the Athletics in a spring exhibition game. I also pitched the Orioles to exhibition victories over the Giants and the Phillies. I knew McGraw was impressed with my pitching and had tried to get a promise from Dunn that when I was put on the market he would get first crack at me. Dunn had played for McGraw in New York and Mac was so sore at Dunnie when I was sold to the Red Sox that in later years he wouldn't even speak to Jack when Duun tried to give him another Oriole southpaw—Lefty Grove.

The way I got it in later years, Dunn first offered Ernie Shore, Ben Egan and me to Connie Mack, telling him we were the cream of his team. Mack was winning the championship again in 1914, but because of Federal League offers to his top players he had a tough season financially. Mack told Dunn, "I'd like to have those fellows but I can't afford them, Jack. You'd better peddle them to some other club that has more money than I have and get the best price you can for them."

The Red Sox, owned by Joe Lannin, were running second to the Athletics that year and trying to make a race of it. Lannin, who was a hotel man in Boston and New York, saved the International League during the Federal League war. He backed clubs in Buffalo and Providence and helped Dunn meet his pay roll in Baltimore. So Dunn, feeling under obligation to Lannin, next offered us to the Boston owner.

The price that Lannin was reported to have paid for us three—Shore, Egan and myself—was given out as $8500. I don't know how they reached the figure, but my price supposedly was $2900. Egan, who didn't last in Boston, was considered to be the high man of the three, with a price tag of $3500. The deal was made on July 8th.

Prior to that I had received two raises. After I started winning games Dunn doubled my salary to $1200 at the end of the first month, and as I kept on winning after a second month he boosted it to $1800. When I moved into the Major Leagues Joe Lannin gave me a new contract at the rate of $2500.

In the meantime I had received some swell offers from the Baltimore Federal League club. They offered me a $10,000 bonus if I would jump and a salary of $10,000. That was an awful temptation for a kid only a few months out of St. Mary's. However, Dunn and the other people high up in organized baseball said that anybody who jumped would be out of Big League baseball for life. As I was a kid just starting I was afraid of hurting my chances and remained loyal to organized baseball. But it was a big laugh about barring the jumpers for life. After the Federal League quit in 1915 all the big names who jumped, Hal Chase,

Chief Bender, Eddie Plank, Lee Magee, Bill McKechnie, Bill Rariden, and other guys like that, all got back with bigger salaries than they had been drawing when they jumped. My decision to stick with Baltimore cost me about $30,000.

When I went to the Red Sox I got the same kind of rough treatment I had experienced in the training camp with the Orioles. Someone must have told them I was a fresh kid who didn't have much respect for big baseball reputations, and I guess some of the old guys let me have it. I suppose I did talk back, but not because I was fresh. I just wanted to show them I was as good as any of the other pitchers Bill Carrigan had. But the thing the older Boston players most resented about me was that I insisted on taking batting practice. One day I came to the park and found that all my bats had been neatly sawed in two. But, generally I got along okay.

Carrigan was nice to me and told me early, "I hear you like to step out, Babe. But you play fair with me and I'll play fair with you." Bill had a lot of great players who had been on the Red Sox World's Champions of 1912. He still had his terrific outfield: Duffy Lewis, Tris Speaker and Harry Hooper. We later had a pretty sweet outfield on the Yankees with Bob Meusel in left, Earle Combs in center, and myself in right. So I am not quite ready to call that Red Sox trio the greatest of all time; but certainly it was one of the best.

The 1914 Red Sox were okay when I joined the club; they had Larry Gardner on third, Everett Scott at short, Steve Yerkes at second, and Dick Hoblitzel on first. Carrigan did much of his own catching, assisted by Forrest Cady and Chet Thomas. The leading pitchers were Dutch Leonard, Joe Wood, George Foster, old Vean Gregg, Hugh Bedient and Ray Collins. That Dutch Leonard wasn't the right-hander now pitching for the Phillies, but an early left-hander who had a great earned-run record in that year.

In my first experience with the Red Sox I lasted only about a month, during which time I pitched in five games, getting credit for two victories against one defeat and making two hits in 10 times at bat. Carrigan worked me for the first time against Cleveland on July 11th and we beat Willie Mitchell, 4 to 3, though Dutch Leonard had to finish the game for me. In seven innings I gave up eight hits, all singles. Joe Jackson, the great Cleveland hitter, made two of the Indian hits. He impressed me more than any other hitter in baseball. Later, when I concentrated more on hitting than on pitching, I would study Shoeless Joe. I noticed that my swing was much the same as his. He took a healthy swing but missed few balls, and when he connected with that dead ball we used in 1914 he could get remarkable distance. I still think Joe Jackson, even though he got into the doghouse, was one of the greatest hitters the sport has ever known. When I read of the present home-run hitting I wonder what Joe Jackson, in his prime, could have done with the modern ball.

As we got into August it was apparent the Red Sox couldn't catch the Athletics. But Joe Lannin's Providence team was in the thick of the pennant fight in the International League. With all of Dunn's stars gone, the Orioles nose-dived into the second division, which gave the Providence team its chance for the pennant. So Lannin sent me over there and I remained for the balance of the season and helped Providence win the pennant. Between the two clubs I won 22 games and lost nine for a percentage of .709. I was feeling my oats but my hat still fitted me.

During my stay with Providence I also hit my first home run in regular competition. I had an odd extra-base record that year—two doubles, 10 triples and one homer.

Though my Providence experience was brief, I shall always remember it because Bill Donovan, one of the finest men of baseball, was my manager. He had been a great pitcher with the old Detroit Tigers when they won pennants and later managed the Yankees just before I joined that team. They used to call him Smiling Bill and Wild Bill, and he was all of that. As a pitcher with Brooklyn early in his career he had been a scatter-arm, which explains why they called him Wild Bill. And they called him Smiling Bill because of his good nature. But he was a smart pitcher and a sound baseball man. He taught me a lot about pitching that came in handy later in my Red Sox experience. Like any kid with a strong arm I liked to get a lot of strike-outs, and I did get 139 in my International League season. But Bill convinced me that a real pitcher works as if he knows he has eight men behind him.

"I used to like to buzz them past their letters, too, when I was a kid," Bill told me. "It was a lot of fun. But if you want to last long in this game as a pitcher you've got to remember your arm is your best friend. Take care of it as you would take care of a good friend. Strike-outs count for outs in the box score; but those other outs at first base or the outfield count just as much in retiring the side."

Another pitcher on that Providence club who soon was to move up with me to the Red Sox was Carl Mays. Our paths were to run together for quite a number of years after that on championship teams on both the Red Sox and Yankees. Carl was a big, stocky fellow from the Middle West with an odd underhand delivery. But he could get a great deal on the ball, and his pitching that year was largely responsible for Providence's championship.

There never was a pitcher quite like Carl. He could throw anything, and with a submarine sweep of his arm that made a hitter think the ball was coming up out of the dirt at him. He was a rough, tough competitor who played for keeps and always had a fine record. But he is remembered today mainly as the man who killed Ray Chapman by breaking his head with a beaner.

3

The First of Ten Pennants

In February, 1915, I became a man, according to my reckoning of time. It made me free of St. Mary's and of Jack Dunn's guardianship. Later statistics showed I was actually only 20 when I, the school and the court thought I was 21. Somehow we got mixed up on the year of my birth, and it wasn't until I took a trip to Japan in 1934 and had to get a birth certificate in order to obtain a passport that I learned I was born in 1895 instead of 1894.

The Red Sox brought me up again after my Providence experience and this time Joe Lannin offered me a contract for $3500. That made me feel like a plutocrat. I was a kid with a healthy appetite and a zest for life who had been in a reform school practically all the time since he was seven years of age. Life looked like a great big lark to me, and after those long hours in St. Mary's tailor shop, baseball was like paradise.

Free from any further legal restraint, I soon became a kid who took his fun where he found it. But I must have tended to business, too, because I was the American League's won-and-lost leader in my first full season in the loop, winning 18 games and losing six for a percentage of .750. No boy who did too much carousing could have won all those ball games. I struck out 112 that year and my earned-run record was 2.44. In 42 games, in some of which I appeared as a pinch hitter, I batted .315 and hit 10 doubles, one triple and four homers.

I learned early that I could hit a ball much harder and farther than the average player, and up in the press box some of the boys were writing that if I could play every day, instead of every fourth, I'd be right up with the home-run leaders of the league. That still was a time when a guy with 10 or 12 homers was called a home-run king.

I used to itch to get to New York in those early days because of the fun I had and the fact that the American League then used the Polo Grounds. I hit the first of my 714* Major League home runs there in 1915 off Jack Warhop, a little guy about the size of that Murry Dickson of the Cardinals. Warhop, part Indian, was a fireman during the off-season. He threw me an underhanded delivery and I put a little fire behind it and knocked it into the right-field stands. It may sound silly now, but in 1915 we thought that was quite a poke. By 1916 I heard that Joe Jackson of the White Sox, the batter who was my model, had hit a ball over the right-field roof at the Polo Grounds. Whenever I came out to the New York field I'd look at that right-field roof and think it would be great if I could knock a ball out of that park.

I don't recall now who was the pitcher, but I got hold of one in the middle of that 1916 season and sent it well over the roof in right center. The writers at that time said it was even a harder and longer hit than Jackson's. So I had the distinction of knocking the second ball over that high Polo Grounds roof. But my thoughts then were still almost entirely on pitching, and I never dreamed that I would make home-run history on that same historic New York field.

*Major League Home Runs (regularly scheduled games)—714
  World Series Home Runs—15
  All Star Games Home Run—1
  Estimated Exhibition Games Home Runs—300.

My 18 victories helped the Red Sox win their fourth American League pennant. We had a terrific race with Detroit and finally finished with 101 victories to their 100. Those 1915 Tigers were the only American League club ever to win 100 games and not win a pennant. Ball clubs really battled in those days, and the Tigers, managed by scrappy Hughey Jennings, and with Ty Cobb having one of his greatest seasons, were one of the really fighting ball clubs of all time. Every time we played them it was a battle. We finally licked them by winning the last two series, first on their home grounds late in August and then in Fenway Park in September.

In the August series, helped by Dutch Leonard, I won a 13-inning, 2 to 1 duel from Bill James and Bernie Boland, and we all got a big laugh when Everett Scott, our weakest hitter, drove in the winning run. The Tigers were berating Scottie about his batting average when he punched out the hit in the 13th that gave us the victory.

There was a lot of spiking and rough stuff in the August series, and the writers with the Boston club wrote all about it, with the result that our fans were riled up when the Tigers came to Fenway Park for a big series, September 16th to 20th. We then had only a slight lead and knew that the series meant the pennant. The crowd especially had it in for Ty Cobb, who had been accused of much of the spiking and rough play in Detroit, and there was a squad of cops in center field to protect Ty from some of the angry bleacherites.

There were few friendships between ballplayers of pennant contenders in those days, even after the ball game was over. We used the roughest kind of language on each other. Of course our special target was Cobb, and there was bad feeling from the first time he went to bat. In one of the games that Mays pitched Ty seemed to think that Carl tossed one at his head and threw his bat at Mays. That started a free-for-all. Cobb was put out of the game and it was necessary for a squad of cops to escort him out of the park so the fans couldn't get at him.

The Tigers won the first game of that final four-game series, but we got going in the second game and won three straight—7 to 2, 1 to 0, and 3 to 2. The pitcher who came up with me from Baltimore, Ernie Shore, won the 1 to 0 game in 12 innings from Harry Coveleskie and I won the final game from George Dauss. We finally clinched the pennant in the last week of the season.

During the middle of the season the Red Sox were lucky to buy Jack Barry, the great Athletic shortstop, from Connie Mack, who was breaking up his club after the Federal League raid of 1914 and 1915. Jack was inserted in our line-up at second base and he and Scottie made a great double-play combination.

That season the Red Sox also picked up Herb Pennock, a promising southpaw kid from the Athletics. Herb later became one of my best friends in baseball, and I consider him one of the greatest pitchers of all time. He only weighed about 165 at his top weight and didn't have the endurance of pitchers like Johnson and Mathewson. But I doubt if there ever was a pitcher who had an easier delivery or was smarter than Herb. We later were teammates on great Yankee teams, and I consider my friendship with Pennock one of my most pleasant experiences in baseball.

I am not trying to fool anybody. I put quite a few gray hairs on Bill Carrigan that 1915 season. He assigned Shore as my roommate at first, thinking that we two Oriole recruits would be congenial. I guess it would have been all right if I had been a little more careful about using Ernie's things. I later got the story from another Red Sox player. After a few weeks of living with me Ernie went to Carrigan and told him he would leave the club unless he drew somebody else for a roommate. He said it was bad enough for me to use his toothbrush but when he complained about it I had said innocently, "That's all right, Ernie, I'm not particular."

After that Bill roomed me with Heinie Wagner, who was then a utility infielder and sort of coach on the club. In fact, we usually had double rooms—Carrigan and Leonard in one of them and Heinie and I in the other. In that way they kept track of us young left-handers after dark, but every now and then we managed to break loose.

They didn't have Sunday ball in Washington in those days. Once when we were in the capital for an idle Sunday I asked Bill's permission to go home to Baltimore to spend some of my time with the folks.

Bill said, "Sure, Babe, run along and be back Monday."

I guess everything would have been all right if my dad hadn't come over from Baltimore to see the Monday ball game. They gave him a box near the Red Sox bench and when he saw me he yelled, "You're a fine son, George, down in this neighborhood and didn't even come home to see me." There wasn't much for me to say, with Bill standing there eyeing me and rocking back and forth on his heels.

I have frequently been asked about my "feud" with Tris Speaker on that 1915 championship Red Sox club. We never really had a scrap and Tris and I are good friends today. Actually there were two cliques on that club. Speaker and Joe Wood were the heads of one and I guess Carrigan and Wagner headed the other. I was on Carrigan's side.

Speaker and Wood were inseparable. They roomed together and always went to the same places. Wood and I had had a little friction on the ball field. The pitchers were warming up before a game one day and a ball thrown by Wood got away from his catcher. It came toward me, but instead of stopping it I bowed my legs and let the ball go through. It didn't amount to much, but Joe yelled something at me and I yelled something back.

At first it was only rough kidding, but pretty soon we were calling each other some riper names. Wood finally said he would take a crack at me and I said, "Let's go to the clubhouse and settle it right now."

I think we did start for the clubhouse, but by that time Carrigan got word of it and pushed us both in opposite directions. The crazy incident did leave some bad feeling, and as Speaker was Joe's pal, naturally he was on Wood's side. But that's the way it is with most baseball fights. You get your hand back and somebody grabs it. You're hot at the time and so is the other guy; but by the next day you usually have forgotten all about it. I never met a ballplayer who really liked to fight.

We played the Phillies in the World Series of 1915. That may give a lot of the present-day fans a laugh, but the Phillies actually did win a pennant once upon a time. Pat Moran, who came from Fitchburg, Mass., was the Phillies' manager—and I think one of the best managers we have ever had in baseball, especially in the difficult job of getting the best out of pitchers. His pitching ace that season was the great Grover Cleveland Alexander, who won 31 games that year, 12 of them shutouts, and had an earned-run record of only 1.22. Before the series Carrigan told us Alexander was going to be tough and that if the Phillies got him one or two runs that probably wonld be enough. Bill told us the Phillies were not a great team, that they weren't in our class. But he said they were a tough, tenacious club and we would have to bear down every minute to beat them. We did win the Series rather easily, four games to one, but the scores of our victories show that Bill was right. We never could let up a moment. Alexander beat Shore in the first game, 3 to 1. But we won the next three games, all by scores of 2 to 1, and then clinched it by winning the final in Philadelphia, 5 to 4. They had some trick bleachers in the Phillies' park, and in that final game Harry Hooper hit two home runs into that section and Duffy Lewis one.

I ate out my heart on the bench in that Series. I was the American League's won-and-lost leader and I naturally expected to pitch. I grabbed Carrigan's lapels before every game and demanded to know when I was to get my chance. However, he started off with Shore and then got winning games out of George Foster and Dutch Leonard. There was a Sunday in between which rested the staff, and then he came back again with Shore and Foster. I just moaned. Before the fourth game I said to Bill, "What the hell does a fellow have to do to get a chance to pitch a World Series game for your club?"

Bill patiently told me Shore had pitched so well in the first game that Ernie deserved another chance, which made sense to me. But I was at him to pitch the fifth game in Philadelphia. This time he told me we had a three-to-one advantage and he thought Foster could wind it up for us after having pitched a three-hitter in landing his first victory. Bill later told me if there had been a sixth game I surely would have pitched it, but we won the Series before any sixth game was necessary.

I did get one chance as a pinch hitter in the Series, and for that I'm thankful because it gives me a chance to say I played in 10 World Series. My opportunity came in the ninth inning of the first game when we were trailing, 3 to 1. Olaf Henriksen batted for Cady and was safe on Luderus' fumble.

Carrigan then called me off the bench and said, "Here's your chance, Babe. This Alexander is no tougher for you than anybody else. Pick out a good ball and hit it."

I did get a good piece of the ball and hit one like

a shot down the first base line. I thought it would go through Luderus but he made up for his error on Olaf by making a great stop, and he beat me to the bag. That was that.

Before leaving the 1915 Red Sox World's Champions I want to say that I think they were baseball's greatest defensive team of all time. We weren't too much of a scoring club and Tris Speaker was our only .300 hitter. Duffy Lewis was the batting star of the series, and Hooper and Larry Gardner were also dangerous. Little Duffy was one of the toughest guys in the clutch in the league, and I know he won many a game for me. About all our pitchers would ask for would be two or three runs, and very often one would be enough. I don't recall how many low-scoring games we won that season, but we won plenty. Winning those three straight 2 to 1 games in the Series seemed natural.

Many years later, Ty Cobb and I were discussing the Tiger and Red Sox clubs of 1915 and our many fights during that red-hot season. Of Carrigan's team Ty said: "On the defense I don't believe that club ever had an equal. You'd get off to a 2 to 1 lead and hold on like grim death. Time after time we'd think we had a rally going in the late innings only to have Scottie or Gardner come up with great stops, or 'Spoke,' Duffy or Hooper pull one of their circus catches in the outfield."

We used to have a steep bank in left field at Fenway Park, and I can still see Duffy Lewis running up that cliff like a mountain goat, reaching out with his gloved or bare hand, and making impossible catches. I'll always remember that.

And during my first year as a Red Sox regular I felt rich enough and old enough (I was 20) to take to myself a wife. She was Helen Woodring, who came originally from Nova Scotia and was a waitress at Landers' Coffee Shop when I first met her. She used to wait on me in the mornings, and one day I said to her, "How about you and me getting married, hon'?"

Helen thought it over for a few minutes and said yes.

I began looking around for a home near Boston, for it had become my home town and I fully expected to spend the next 20 years there, pitching for the Red Sox.

4

I Win 23—Twice

I won 23 games for the 1916 Red Sox and came back in 1917 to win 23 more. I knew what the top of the world felt like to sit on, even though I wasn't earning half the money which a bench-warming utility man makes today.

In 1916, Harry Coveleskie, the big Tiger left-hander, tied my 23 wins, but I was the league's earned-run leader with 1.75. And during that same year I got one of the biggest thrills of my life, and that goes for my longest home runs, too. In a tough game with Detroit the Tigers filled the bases with none out, but I pitched my way out of the hole by striking out Ty Cobb, Sam Crawford and Bobbie Veach. It made almost as much commotion as Carl Hubbell's feat of later years when he struck out Lou Gehrig, Al Simmons, Jimmy Foxx, Joe Cronin and myself in the All-Star Game of 1934.

Every once in a while a young baseball writer will write that I wasn't a pitcher but a thrower. I read not so long ago that I didn't bother with signals; I just had a strong powerful arm and tried to blow down the hitters by throwing the ball past them.

Maybe so, but how do they think I got that 1.75 earned run average and finished ahead of Walter Johnson, Ernie Shore, Coveleskie, Carl Mays, Joe Bush and Bob Shawkey? What's more, in 1916 the American League was a very tough league. It was just before the clubs began losing players to the services and just after they took back the Federal League jumpers.

And the young writers just didn't know Carrigan. Bill was a keen student of the strengths and weaknesses of every hitter in the league; whether he was behind the plate or on the bench he "called" every pitch thrown. He'd hit the ceiling if any of his pitchers tried to pitch his own game instead of following Bill's game. He could get just about as tough as anybody I ever met. We didn't call him "Rough" Carrigan for nothing.

I have often been asked to name the greatest manager I worked under. People know I played for two smart New York managers who won a lot of pennants, Miller Huggins and Joe McCarthy. But I always surprise them when I answer, "Bill Carrigan."

One reason why I rate Bill on top is the way he kept the Red Sox up front after we lost Tris Speaker, our great center fielder and best hitter, just before the opening of the 1916 season.

The Federal League war was over and stars who were getting big salaries as the result of Federal League offers had to take cuts that made them scream. I got the same as I did in 1915—$3500—but "Spoke" was cut in half, from $18,000 to $9,000.

Wood, Speaker's pal, won 14 games for us in 1915. He had a sore arm most of the time, and Lannin did one of those major amputations on Joe's contract. Wood refused to show up at our Hot Springs training camp. "Spoke" was there, but he was dissatisfied and still hadn't signed a contract by the time we got back to Boston to open the season with the Athletics.

On opening day we heard the bad news. Tris was sold to Cleveland for $50,000, and two young players nobody then knew much about—Sam Jones, who became a great pitcher, and Fred Thomas, a third baseman. It was a tremendous deal. Today it would be like selling Joe DiMaggio without warning, or pulling Ted Williams out of Boston the year after he hit .400.

About the time Lannin sold Speaker to Cleveland he bought another outfielder, Clarence Walker, from the Browns. Walker had a tight walk and we used to call him "Tillie." Later in the same season the Red Sox brought up Chick Shorten from their Minor League farm in Providence. Chick and "Tillie" then took turns in playing center field.

Lannin was doing the best he could but we all felt that Speaker's sale had pulled the rug from under us. As a pitcher I knew what it meant having Tris out there in the outfield.

Some of us were talking it over and feeling sorry for ourselves, when Carrigan overheard the conversation. He broke in on us sharply.

"All right, we lost Speaker," he barked. "But we're still a tight ball club. We've got good pitching, good fielding, and we'll hit well enough. If you guys stop your——moaning and get down to business we can win that pennant again."

I know how the pep talk reacted on me. I suddenly remembered that the $3780 check I got out of the 1915 World Series was more than my season's pay, and I wanted another to match it. Without Speaker we hustled even harder and we worked ourselves into another pennant. It wasn't easy by a long shot. Detroit fought us hard most of the way, but the White Sox, managed by Clarence Rowland, came fast late in the season and we had to go all out to finish two games ahead of them. We were a great ball club—Speaker or no Speaker. This time we knocked over the Brooklyn Dodgers, four games to one, just as we had belted the Phillies in 1915. And losing that one game wasn't too bad, because it was to Jack Coombs, the ex-Athletic star. I said to Dutch Leonard after the game, "If we had to lose that one I'm glad it was to an old American Leaguer." I don't know how much comfort it was to Dutch.

As in 1915, we played our home games during the 1916 Series at Braves Field because of its larger seating capacity. We opened at home on Saturday, October 7th, and Ernie Shore almost blew a 6 to 1 lead in the ninth. The Dodgers scored four runs and had the bases filled when Carrigan called in Carl Mays to relieve Ernie. Jake Daubert, who was the National League's best hitter, then drove a hot grounder to Scottie in deep short. I'll never forget Scottie's long throw across the infield to Dick Hoblitzel on first. Jake was called out on a very close decision. Wilbert Robinson, the fat Brooklyn manager, fell off the bench after Hobbie caught Scottie's long peg. Uncle Robby had leaned forward to follow the course of the ball and went on his face when he saw Jake beaten to the bag by inches.

We didn't have Sunday ball in Boston in those days, and I got my first World Series pitching chance in the second game, on Monday. Robby pitched Sherry Smith, a Georgia left-hander, against me, and we had one of the greatest World Series battles ever put into the book. Our 14-inning game, which I won, 2 to 1, still is the longest of all World Series games. It was so dark at the close that even the sharpest eyes on the field could hardly follow the ball.

I would have had a shutout if Walker and Lewis hadn't run into each other while trying to get a line drive by Hi Myers in the first inning. Either outfielder could have played the ball for a single, but when they crashed they hit the grass and the ball rolled to the outfield fence. Myers ran around the bases for an inside-the-park home run.

I drove in the run that tied the score for us in the third inning. They were playing Everett Scott close, and he pushed a line drive between Wheat and Myers and pulled up at third base for a triple. I then grounded to George Cutshaw at second base and Scottie crossed the plate with the tying run.

From there on it was a dogfight as inning after inning went by without a score. Both Smitty and I were in top form, and only a few men reached base on both sides. It was getting quite dark when we played the 13th inning, and it was darker than that when Brooklyn went to bat in the 14th. Bill Klem, the umpire, always has maintained that the 14th inning never should have been started.

Anyway, I got Brooklyn out in the first half of the 14th and Hobbie opened for us by drawing a base on balls. Duffy Lewis sent him down to second on a sacrifice bunt. Hoblitzel was slow, so Carrigan called on Mike McNally to run for him, and on a hunch sent Del Gainer, a right-handed hitter, to bat for Larry Gardner. Larry was one of our best hitters, but Bill felt that in the darkness Gainer might have a better chance to see Smith's left-handed fast ball. We heard the crack of the bat, and the next thing we knew Wheat was trying to find the ball out in left field, and a moment later Mike McNally was streaking down the third base line and across the plate with our winning run.

I know it was one of the happiest moments of my life. I had been waiting for two years to pitch against the National League champions, and I think I convinced Carrigan that I could hold them as well as any other pitcher on his staff. In the midst of the clubhouse roughhouse I said to Bill, "I told you a year ago I could take care of those National League bums for you, but you never gave me a chance."

But Bill was too happy to care much what I said about his judgment on starting pitchers, because he hugged me and yelled, "Forget it, Babe. You surely made monkeys of them today."

Scottie again played grand ball for us at short, as did Hal Janvrin, a Boston high-school boy, who was substituting for Jack Barry at second base. Both were all over the infield, and some of their great stops made it possible for me to carry the game into the 14th inning.

I never did get a chance to work again in that Series. I was down to pitch the sixth game if there had been one, but we polished them off in five games. Carl Mays lost the first game we played in Brooklyn to Coombs, 4 to 3, but Dutch Leonard won the next day, 6 to 2. We then went back to Boston, and Ernie Shore wound it up for us on Columbus Day with an easy 4 to 1 victory in which he gave up only three hits.

Brooklyn played a terrible fielding game all through the Series, which helped us over the rough spots. The shortstop for the Dodgers was Ivan Olson, who had played in the American League with Cleveland. Ivy had a horrible Series and we didn't do anything to help him. We used to yell out, "When in doubt hit to Ivy." We had him crazy before it was over.

But I'll say this for him—he had as much courage as any player I've ever known. He wasn't the best fielder in the world but he never backed out of a fight. At one stage of the Series he said he'd lick our whole ball club. Of course, we only greeted him with laughs, and the more we laughed the madder he became, and the madder he became the worse he played.

Mike McNally, who scored the winning run in my 14-inning game, carried a box score for years showing that he once batted for me. Mike, who now looks like a barrel and is President of the Red Sox Scranton club, was a skinny kid as a ballplayer. He didn't weigh 150 and hit little more. However, one day we were taking a bad beating, and I went to the clubhouse in the ninth inning not thinking that they would get around to me in the batting order. But we got really going, and when it came my turn to bat I was in a shower. Carrigan put in McNally to bat for me.

Mike carried the clipping of that box score until you could hardly see the type, it had been thumbed by so many unbelieving people. I saw him show it to some sports writers one day, after we both became members of the Yankees, and I said, "Mike, if you show that box score to anyone again I'll make you eat it."

The Red Sox took another heavy blow at the end of the 1916 Series. During the latter part of the season we had heard reports that Carrigan was going to quit baseball and go up to his home town, Lewiston, Me., where he owned a bank. At the start the players didn't pay much attention to it. We thought that Bill was getting ready to put the bee on Joe Lannin for a long-term contract. But after our World Series celebration in the clubhouse Bill shook hands with all of us, thanked us for the way we had served him, and wished us luck the rest of our playing days. Just like that. It had never happened before and it has never happened since.

It was a big blow to me. I not only had a great respect for the man himself, but I had a kid's admiration for a great baseball general. I knew how much he had helped me and in my mind began wondering how well I would succeed under another manager.

Not only did Carrigan leave the team after the 1916 World Series, but shortly before Christmas Joe Lannin sold the Red Sox to Harry Frazee, a New York theatrical man.

They'll never build any monuments to Frazee in Boston. In fact, until Tom Yawkey rebuilt the Red Sox it wasn't healthy to mention Frazee's name in Boston. He ruined one of the American League's great ball clubs by systematically selling star after star to the rich owners of the Yankees, Col. Jake Ruppert and Col. T. L. Huston.

Frazee knew the theater but he didn't know much about baseball. He said once that no ballplayer was worth more than $8000 a year. "Why, I don't pay any of my best actors more than that." I want to be fair to Harry, however, and say that in his early years in Boston he really tried to build up the club rather than to tear it down. He bought the club on a shoestring, and it wasn't until after Lannin, the former owner, began to press him for unpaid notes that he began disposing of his stars.

The first thing Frazee did on taking over was to try to induce Bill Carrigan to change his mind. But Bill seemed set. He not only owned the bank in Lewiston, but a flock of Maine movie houses, and felt they required all his time and attention. Harry then promoted Jack Barry, our second baseman and former Athletic star, to the management of the club. Jack wasn't a Carrigan, but he was a smart, college-educated man who had learned his baseball under the old master, Connie Mack. For years after the first World War Barry was baseball coach at Holy Cross.

With Jack directing the club we made a good fight of it as far as Labor Day, 1917. Up until that time it was touch and go between the two Soxes, the White and the Red. But Chicago spurted in September, kept pulling away, and eventually beat us out by nine games.

As I said before, I won 23 games for the second place 1917 club, as I had done for our pennant winner of 1916, and again was one of the pitching leaders of both major leagues. But I was lucky. I nearly ruined even my chance to appear in enough games to win as many as 23. On June 23rd of that season, in a game against Washington, I blew my top and punched an umpire, Brick Owens. It wasn't a love pat. I really socked him—right on the jaw. That game is in the record books today, but I'm glad my part in it isn't mentioned.

I pitched to only one batsman, Eddie Foster, the Senators' lead-off man. Brick Owens called four straight balls on me, and though I've cooled off a lot in the 30 years since then, I still insist that three of the four should have been strikes. I growled at some of the early balls, but when he called the fourth one on me I just went crazy. I rushed up to the plate and I said, "If you'd go to bed at night, you so-and-so, you could keep your eyes open long enough in the daytime to see when a ball goes over the plate."

Brick could dish it, too.

"Shut up, you lout," he said, "or I'll throw you out of the game."

"Throw me out of this game and I'll punch you right on the jaw," I bellowed.

Brick looked at me coldly.

"You're out of this game right now," he said, with a big jerk of his thumb.

I hauled off and hit him, but good. Chet Thomas, our catcher, Barry and other players tore us apart and hustled me to the clubhouse.

Ban Johnson, then the American League's president, was very easy on me. I was fined only $100 and suspended for ten days. They'd put you in jail today for hitting an umpire. Ben Chapman, who played with me on the Yankees, and Burleigh Grimes were put out of the game for a year for taking a punch at umpires of a later day.

But my stupid act wasn't the reason why the game made the record books. Ernie Shore, with little time to warm up, came in to relieve me and retired the next 26 Washington hitters in order. Foster, the man who reached base on me in the first, was thrown out while trying to steal. So they gave Shore credit for pitching a perfect game. It is one of only six perfect games pitched in the recorded history of baseball.

I look back at another game I pitched for the 1917 Red Sox with much more pride. One of the most beloved sports writers of all time, Tim Murnane, died early in 1917 and the Boston writers talked the management into playing a benefit game for his widow.

Tim was one of the grand old men of the sport, a real baseball pioneer. He had played for the Boston National League club in 1876, the year the National League was born. When his legs gave out he became a baseball writer on the Boston *Globe,* and by the time I got to Boston Tim was the baseball authority of New England. If Tim said something was right or wrong, there was no argument. His was the last word. He was a handsome old fellow with a big shock of white hair and laughing Irish eyes. He was also the first to predict that I'd make my mark in the game. I don't know what I did to justify it, but during that month I served with the 1914 Red Sox Tim wrote that if I watched my step I'd take my place "with the greatest left-handers of all time."

The Boston sports writers rounded up one of the greatest teams ever assembled to play the Red Sox on Tim Murnane Day. When I see some of the clubs that are picked for the All-Star teams nowadays I wonder what chance they'd have against the All-Star team that took the field against us in that benefit game. That All-Star line-up read: Rabbit Maranville, Braves, shortstop; Ray Chapman, Indians, second base; Ty Cobb, Tigers, center field; Tris Speaker, Indians, left field; Joe Jackson, White Sox, right field; Buck Weaver, White Sox, third base; Steve O'Neill, Indians, catcher; Urban Shocker, Browns, Howard Ehmke, Tigers, and Walter Johnson, Senators, pitchers.

Jack Barry gave me the honor of pitching against this great team. I still don't know how I did it, but I shut them out with three hits in five innings. Then George Foster allowed none in the last four, and the Red Sox won the game, 2 to 0. The score was 0 to 0 until the eighth when Duffy Lewis broke it up by tripling off Walter Johnson, the greatest pitcher I ever saw, with a man on base.

In my three successful years with the Red Sox I had plenty of fun and did my share of hell-raising, but often my thoughts went back to St. Mary's and to Brother Matthias and Brothers Paul, Albert, and Gilbert. I knew they loved baseball and were watching the progress in the Big Leagues of their ex-catcher and tailor's apprentice. I recall my joy in winning my first World Series game—that 2 to 1, 14-inning victory over Sherry Smith—and the messages from Brother Matthias and the boys still in the school with whom I had played. And I still treasure the only fan letter I got during the 1914 season. It was from Brother Matthias and it read, "You're doing fine, George. I'm proud of you."

I had kept in close contact with the school, and even then, before I was in the important money, had sent it some contributions. I wanted it to share in my new prosperity. The kids I left behind took on a new importance for me, and I guess that feeling was the beginning of what smarter fellows than I call a social consciousness. But all I knew then, and for that matter now, is that there is nothing in this country as important as our kids.

Kids happen to like me, feel natural around me. I'm the same around them. It isn't just a case of giving out autographs. I've always felt cleaner after a session with kids. Wherever they've gathered, they've turned my thoughts back to St. Mary's and my early days in that institution.

At the start of my baseball career kids weren't autograph hunters to the degree they are now. They just hung around ball park entrances to stare bug-eyed at the big leaguers. If you gave them a friendly pat on the back or said, "Hello, kid," it made them happy. I suppose that's how I came to greet everybody, "Hello, kid," in my later years. I saw so many faces, of all colors and ages, that wished me well, it was difficult to remember names. When it came to remembering names, whether of ball players, sports writers, or fans, I was no Jim Farley.

The better known I became around Boston as a double 23-game winner and a hitting pitcher the more I realized that I could earn a comfortable living on the side. I put some of my money in a small Boston cigar factory that put out a Babe Ruth cigar, and I smoked them until I was blue in the face. They sold like hotcakes and some of their critics swore they were.

5

My Proudest Achievement

The United States entered the first World War just before the start of the 1917 season, but the draft law was slow in getting into operation and baseball lost comparatively few men in that first war season. Hank Gowdy, the Boston Braves catcher, was one of the first to go. But on the whole the 1917 teams went through the season with their full rosters.

However, the country began to become more aware of the war during the winter of 1917–1918, and many of the Red Sox went into uniform. Most of them picked the Navy, including manager Jack Barry, Dutch Leonard, Duffy Lewis, Mike McNally, Herb Pennock, Ernie Shore, Del Gainer, Hal Janvrin, Jimmy Walsh and Fred Thomas. Dick Hoblitzel, our first baseman, started the 1918 season but he went into the Army after a month's play. Like a lot of others, I was deferred as a married man, joined a National Guard unit and kept playing.

Barry's enlistment put Frazee on quite a spot. He had lost Carrigan shortly after buying the club a year before and now he again found it necessary to dig up a new manager. Ed Barrow at the time was president of the International League but Frazee never was a shy guy. Barrow was more than experienced; he had managed the Detroit Tigers and a number of Minor League clubs—Toronto, Montreal, Indianapolis, and Paterson. At Paterson he found and developed the great Honus Wagner and sold him to Louisville, which then was in the National League.

Barrow was a two-fisted, hard-boiled soul who had built up a reputation in baseball as a man who not only knew how to use his fists but liked the idea. He was hot-tempered; and though it was Barrow who helped make me what I became in the game, we had our share of clashes. Barrow was a strict disciplinarian. I was still at the age when I resented anyone pulling the bit too tight on me. As it turned out, we became good friends. We certainly had enough time to mend our differences. Except for 1920, we were together from 1918 until I left the Yankees early in 1935.

I had my earliest run-in with him on Decoration Day in 1918. We played a game in Washington on a Saturday. There was no game scheduled for Sunday, but we were to play morning and afternoon holiday games in Philadelphia on Monday. On the way from Washington to Philadelphia, on Sunday, I hopped off the train at Baltimore, for I had a sudden longing to see my sister. There wasn't time to ask permission of Ed or anybody else.

When he discovered I had left the train, Ed hit the ceiling and decided I had gotten off to go back to Washington, where I had some gay companions. He sent Heinie Wagner, the Boston coach, to look for me and the two of us finally showed up Monday just before the morning game. Ed was really steaming.

Barrow called all the players together, and before the entire team he gave me the worst bawling out of my entire career. It was a double-barreled beaut. He threatened to knock my block off if I ever left the club again without permission. I was a hothead, too, and yelled that I was going to leave the Red Sox and jump to a shipyard team at Fore River, Massachusetts. They had a pretty good ball club there and had made good offers to me and to other major leaguers. Like most baseball arguments it soon died down. Barrow called me up to his room that night, talked me out of it, and I went on to have a great season under his management.

We won the pennant again in 1918, the shortest baseball season on record. Secretary of War Newton D. Baker closed down the season on Labor Day in keeping with the country's "work or fight" order. What we were doing naturally came under the head of neither.

Frazee was called the "Red Sox wrecker" later on, but some of his war deals made our 1918 pennant possible. We never could have won without the players he obtained from the Athletics: first baseman Stuffy McInnis, catcher Wally Schang, pitcher Joe Bush, and outfielder Amos Strunk. To fill Jack Barry's place at second he obtained Dave Shean from the Cincinnati Reds. George Whiteman, an outfielder, was purchased from the Toronto club.

In the general mix-up, they made a part-time outfielder out of a 23-game winner named Ruth. We had a fine defensive club and Barrow got a lot of good pitching out of Carl Mays, Joe Bush, Sam Jones and myself that year. But we were light at bat, especially against right-hand pitching. We started the season with Hoblitzel at first and Stuffy McInnis at third; but after Hobbie went into the Army McInnis returned to first and a lot of guys not in McInnis' class took turns in playing third.

I had been getting some long hits as a pitcher, despite the soggy ball of 1918. One day that year, Barrow called me to his room. I didn't know what was up, but assumed I had burned him up again. But as I walked in, I found him smiling.

"Sit down, Babe. Make yourself at home," he invited.

We talked about this and that, while I sweated it

out. But finally there was a tense silence. Ed cleared his throat.

"Babe," he said, "everybody knows you're a big fellow, healthy and strong. Why can't you take your turn in the box and still play the outfield on days when you're not pitching."

I didn't have to think about it very long.

"I'll try, Ed, and see how it goes," I said.

From then on I was in the line-up every day a right-handed pitcher was against us. I played sometimes at first base, but mostly I was in left field. When a south-paw worked against us Barrow usually tried to maneuver the staff so that I would pitch against him. Occasionally I'd get an afternoon off, but I'd spend it in the bull pen available for pinch-hitting purposes, or I would be called in to relieve. All this was before anybody heard of a baseball union. I guess I just liked the game.

I didn't turn from a pitcher to an outfielder over-night, as some people seem to think. It was a gradual sort of thing, and I guess the old German Kaiser deserves an assist in my conversion. Barrow probably would have been committed someplace if he had worked a 23-game winner in the outfield when he still had such players as Duffy Lewis, Chick Shorten and Jimmy Walsh on his team. But 1918 was one of those makeshift seasons. It was like 1944 and 1945 during the last war, when a manager had to make the best of the material he had left on his hands.

At that time I would have preferred playing first base during games in which I didn't pitch. But Stuffy McInnis was tops. So I just had to learn how to play the outfield. At first, some of the writers kidded Barrow about playing me in left field. They even made bets I'd be hit on the head by a fly ball before the season's end. But I had been chasing after flies ever since Brother Matthias used to bat them out to us down at St. Mary's with one big hand, and I didn't do so badly. I wasn't any Duffy Lewis out there at the start, but I gradually improved and before the season was over nobody was trying to hit to left or taking any extra bases on me. I loved to throw that ball to any base, from any part of the garden.

Between pitching, playing first base and the outfield I appeared in 95 games that season and, oddly enough, cracked out 95 hits. I hit for an even .300.

I always got a kick out of hitting a ball. But it was a pleasanter feeling to know that the more I played the sharper my batting eye got. I was winning a lot of respect up there at the plate and getting the first of what turned out to be a record 2056 bases on balls, most of them intentional. And occasionally I was teeing off on that squash and getting distance which some of the sports writers of that era apparently found hard to believe.

In my 95 games I collected 26 doubles, 11 triples and 11 home runs. Today the bat boy hits 11 home runs, but in 1918 it was good enough to get me a tie with "Tillie" Walker of the Athletics as the leading home-run hitter of the American League.

Even though Secretary of War Baker and General Crowder, who was in charge of the draft in the first World War, ordered the big leagues to close their season on Labor Day, the two championship clubs, the Red Sox and the Cubs, were given a special dispensation to play the World Series in early September.

We were to start the Series in Chicago on September 4th and play at Comiskey Park, the American League field, because it then had a much greater capacity than the old Federal League park in Chicago, now Wrigley Field. We felt that gave us an edge because we played 11 games there every year.

It rained on the opening day of the series, and I was sitting around the hotel, restlessly, when Barrow called me

"Babe," he said, "everybody is expecting me to

start with Carl Mays tomorrow with you in left field. Jim Vaughn is almost sure to start for the Cubs. So I am going to cross them and pitch you. I'd rather have you pitch against another left-hander and play Whiteman in left, because he's a right-handed hitter. Don't say anything about this. I want it to be a surprise to the Cubs when you start to warm up before the game."

I was pleased with this opening game assignment. I guess I was still a pitcher at heart and I looked forward to grappling with big Vaughn, who had formerly been an American Leaguer with the Yankees. My win-and-lose mark had dropped to 13 and 6 that season, because of the short schedule and my work at other positions, but I was cocky enough to believe I could beat Vaughn.

Well, Big Vaughn, who weighed 220 pounds, and I had quite a battle. He slipped only once, and I worked my way out of two tough spots and came out on top by the score of 1 to 0. Barrow's judgment was great. Little Georgie Whiteman, who played left field, knocked out a single in the fourth inning which advanced Dave Shean from first to third. Fred Mitchell, the Chicago manager, then tried to place his fielders for Stuffy McInnis, who invariably hit to left field. But no defense could ever really stop Stuffy, a consistent .300 hitter. He lined a single over third baseman Deal's head, scoring Shean with the run that gave me the victory.

Twice during the game I was in holes where a single would have beaten me, but each time I made a fall guy out of Charlie Pick, a former American Leaguer who had played with the Athletics. I got him to pop up with two outs and the bases filled in the first inning.

Barrow never gets tired of talking about something that happened in that game. I've said before that names and faces of players often stumped me. I honestly didn't know one from another, half the time. I wasn't as bad as some of the kidding sports writers made me out to be but this one really happened.

While we were going over the Chicago hitters in our clubhouse before the game Barrow called special attention to Les Mann, one of the Cub outfielders. He was a chunky little guy, and while he never hit much against right-handed pitching he was poison to left-handers. Turning to me, Ed said, "Now, this man is tough against left-handers, Babe, and any time he comes up in a pinch I want you to be careful. In fact, it won't do any harm to dust him off a bit, for he takes a heavy toe hold on the plate."

Well, the game got under way and the first Chicago batter was a rugged little left-handed hitter who just about crowded the plate off the diamond. I threw one at him, to back him off, and accidentally hit him in the middle of the forehead.

"I guess I took care of that Mann guy for you," I said to Ed at the end of the inning.

He laughed so he almost fell off the bench.

"Babe, you wouldn't know General Grant if he walked up there with a bat," he howled.

It seems I had hit Max Flack instead of Mann.

Counting my 13 scoreless innings in the 1916 Series against Brooklyn, I now had 22 consecutive World Series innings in which I goose-egged the National League. I didn't do it, but I was in a mood to send Brother Matthias a wire saying, "Thanks again for convincing me that I wasn't a catcher."

It was a great Series in 1918 and the two teams exchanged a lot of rough talk. We had some accomplished jockeys on both benches. Heinie Wagner on our side rode Vaughn hard in the first game and Otto Knabe, who was utility infielder on the Cubs, threw the harpoon into Joe Bush when he pitched later in the Series. At one time the exchanges between Wagner and Vaughn became so hot that Heinie charged the

Cub bench to get at the big left-hander. They really let Heinie have it. His face was well bruised and he was covered with blood, mud and water when the umpires pulled him out of the brawl. I tried to get in the scrap myself but Barrow held me back, and said, "I want you to pitch in this Series, Babe, not fight."

Despite the feuding, the players got together and almost pulled a strike before the fifth game. Because of the war and a kind of ceiling on costs they didn't raise prices in this Series and the gate was small. We knew that the players' shares would be peanuts. But what made it especially bad for the Red Sox and the Cubs was that this was the first year in which the owners voted to give purses to the second-, third-, and fourth-place players. We felt that was all right, but not under wartime conditions, when baseball salaries were off.

Hooper was our ambassador and Les Mann served the same way for the Cubs. They went to see the three officials who then made up the old National Commission—Garry Hermann, Ban Johnson and John Heydler—and offered them two plans. Hooper and Mann asked the Commission either to hold back the purses to first-division players in 1918, or to give a flat sum of $1500 to the winning players in the World Series and $1000 to the losers. The Commissioners practically threw out our bargainers.

So before the fifth game at Fenway Park the players refused to go out on the field.

There was a big crowd in the stands that day, too, and they got sorer the longer we stayed inside. "Honey" Fitzgerald, the Mayor of Boston, tried to talk the Boston players into going on with the game. When we refused, he called the police riot squad. Finally, our committee met again with the three Commissioners in the umpires' room and Ban Johnson, who was feeling no pain, convinced Harry Hooper, our representative, that we should go on with the

game. It got started an hour late after "Honey" Fitzgerald had made a speech at the plate in behalf of
the players. In that pre-loudspeaker era the Mayor,
shouting and turning, told the fans who could hear
him that we had decided to play for the sake of the
public and the wounded men in the stands.

We finally won the Series, four games to two, and
each of our games was won by one run: 1 to 0, 2 to
1, 3 to 2, and 2 to 1. Mays was credited with two
victories and I was credited with two, though I didn't
finish the second game. However, I'm still prouder of
my achievement of pitching 29 consecutive World Series scoreless innings than I am of my subsequent
home-run records with the Yankees. The record still
stands. It beat that of the great Mathewson, who
pitched 28 consecutive World Series innings with the
Giants, 27 of them in his three shutouts against the
Athletics in 1905 and one more inning against the A's
in 1911.

As a matter of fact, I might have gone on further
with this goose-egg chain if I hadn't been pitching
under great difficulty in the fourth game. We had a
second-string left-hander on our club by the name of
Kenny. He and I used to go in for a lot of roughhous-
ing and were always clowning with each other. We'd
grapple and box and roll all over the floor.

On the train ride back to Boston for the fourth
game we started it again. I took a swing at Kenny,
but he ducked and I hit the knuckles of my left hand
on the steel wall of the car. The middle finger of my
left hand became swollen to three times its normal
size.

Barrow was wild when he saw it.

"You damn fool!" he bellowed. "You know I've
picked you to pitch the fourth game and you go and
bust up your hand that way. Don't you want to win
this Series?"

I replied, "It's okay, Ed. I'll be in there pitching for you tomorrow, if you still want me to."

However, as early as the first inning I knew that I was working under a bad handicap. The swollen finger prevented me from getting my regular grip on the ball. I couldn't get the right twist when I threw my curve. I still don't know how I got as far as I did. But I blanked them for seven innings to bring my total up to 29 before they scored two runs on me in the eighth and tied the score.

I had been responsible for our two runs with my first World Series hit. It came in the fourth inning, which was our lucky inning all through that Series. Shean started it with a walk and stole second. Strunk flied out, but George Tyler, the Cub pitcher, then walked Whiteman, putting two runners on base. Stuffy McInnis forced Shean at third, and that brought me to the plate.

As I left the bench Barrow said, "I don't know whether they'll let you hit or not, Babe. But if they pitch to you, you can win your own game. I know you can do it."

Some of the sports writers who were pulling for the National League wrote later that Fred Mitchell, the Cub manager, pulled a bad boner by ordering Tyler to pitch to me. But no manager likes to give an intentional pass with runners on first and second. Besides, I hadn't made a World Series hit up to this time in ten times at bat.

I guess I was due.

I thought Tyler intended to pass me when he served up three straight balls, all quite wide of the plate. Then he slipped me a slow curve. It wasn't good baseball for me to hit at a three and nothing pitch, but Barrow had told me to win my own game and I took a cut at it. I missed it about a foot and the crowd groaned. I let the next one go by, but Brick Owens, the umpire I had slugged in 1917, called it strike two.

Tyler looked me over for a long time, then tried to sneak over a fast ball for a third strike. But I was doing some looking myself. The ball came over waist high. I swung from my heels and rammed it far over Flack's head in right field for a triple, scoring Whiteman and McInnis. I was left on third base when Flack pulled down Scottie's long fly, but it didn't seem to matter. Barrow was beating me on the back, and I had a 2 to 0 lead.

After the Cubs tied the score on me in the eighth they sent in Phil Douglas, their big spitball pitcher, to face us in the second half, and we promptly got the lead back in our half. Wally Schang batted for Sam Agnew, our other catcher, and knocked out a pinch single. It didn't take him long to score as one of Douglas' spitballs slipped through Bill Killefer's glove for a passed ball and Wally ran to second. Hooper sacrificed, and when Douglas threw the wet ball into right field, trying for a play at first, Schang scored.

That run again gave us a 3 to 2 lead, and I would have given anything to have been able to finish that game. But after I walked Fred Merkle, the old Giant, and Rollie Zieder, the first two men up in the ninth, Barrow pulled me off the slab. However, instead of sending me to the showers he sent me to left field, and called in Joe Bush to retire the side.

A great play by Stuffy McInnis really saved the ball game for me. As Wortman tried to sacrifice, Stuffy made one of those Hal Chase plays by running almost to the plate for the bunt and threw to Thomas, our third baseman, for a forced play on Merkle. The game was over a moment later when Barber, a pinch hitter, grounded to Scottie, who turned it into a double play. It gave me my third World Series pitching victory— and my last one.

6

Birth of a
New Home-Run Record

We were back to peacetime baseball in 1919. The game came back with a loud bang, and the entire tempo of my life—and career—suddenly was stepped up. This was the season I knocked all existing home-run records out of the books with 29, an unheard-of total for that day. It was a hectic year, not only for me but for those who were trying to handle me.

I had been paid $5000 for 1917, and $7000 for 1918. After helping the Red Sox win another pennant and the World Series in the last war year I wanted more money from Frazee. I put my price at $10,000 and felt I had it coming. But Frazee yelled as if I were trying to rob the cash drawer at the old Frazee Theater in New York. For $10,000 he said he'd expect at least John Barrymore. I asked him what good Barrymore's profile would be with the bases filled in a tight ball game.

My 11 home runs in 1918 and my 29 consecutive scoreless World Series innings had gotten me a lot of national publicity, and a kind of manager, named Johnny Igo. Igo thought it would be a great idea, and a profitable one, if I became a boxer.

I was certainly big enough, and strong enough, and he figured that if I could knock out home runs I could knock out the Willards, Fultons and Johnsons of that day. Igo was nice enough not to mention a young challenger for Willard's title named Jack Dempsey.

I worked out in a Boston gym that winter, and a

Boston promoter offered me $5000 to fight Gunboat Smith. I wasn't yet in the big baseball dough and doubted if I ever would get there under Frazee. My World Series share in 1918 was only a little over $1000. I wanted that five grand and I was willing to fight for it. I okayed the match.

McInnis also became a holdout about that time and that's when Barrow intervened. He got both of us to go to Frazee's office in New York, and after some haggling I signed a two-year contract calling for $10,000 a year with Frazee still moaning that no ballplayer was worth that kind of money. And as soon as I signed, Barrow took me aside and said, "Now, get that crazy idea of fighting out of your thick skull. You concentrate on baseball, and if there's any fighting to be done you fight for Red Sox ball games."

We trained in Tampa that spring, and hooked up many times with the Giants of John McGraw, who were getting into shape at Gainesville, Fla. And it was in a game between the Sox and the Giants at the old Tampa race-track diamond that I hit a home run that is still talked about.

Every now and then I'm still asked whether it was the longest ball I ever hit. I don't know, really, but I sure hit that ball! The pitcher was a big, lanky guy who had gone to Columbia University in New York, and they called him "Hail Columbia" George Smith. I don't remember what he threw me but it looked awful fat coming up there.

There was a little rail fence out in deepest right field. The ball I hit never rose more than 30 feet off the ground, and Boss Youngs, the classic Giant outfielder, rode out with it until he looked like a little boy running after a bird. The ball cleared the fence and then kept rolling. Paul Shannon, the Boston baseball writer, and Frank Graham, now of the New York *Journal-American*, got out a tape measure the next morning and measured it. It was nearly 500 feet to the fence and 600 feet to where the ball stopped rolling.

Some of the writing guys, especially those with the Giants, began to get pretty excited about that hit and started speculating on how many home runs I'd hit if Barrow played me every day. McGraw overheard them and said, "If he does, that big bum will hit into a hundred double plays before the season is over."

McGraw and I were good friends later on, especially when Christy Walsh used to syndicate both our columns. But the remark came back to me, and whenever I'd get a long hit off one of McGraw's pitchers that spring, or in later years, I'd yell at him, "How's that for a double-play ball, Mac?"

The Giants and the Red Sox came out of Florida together, and we had one of the roughest training series I ever played in. They had Larry Doyle, Heinie Zimmerman, Benny Kauff and Arthur Fletcher, who later came to the Yankees as a coach. I don't think baseball ever had a better coach, or a sharper tongue, than Fletcher.

Baseball changes through the years. It gets milder. Take those Giants, for instance. I don't know whether they wanted to show us how tough they were, but they played every game as though a $5000 World Series check was riding on it.

There was one game in Raleigh in which most of our bigger men, including myself, had called it a day and already were in the showers when Larry Doyle, the Giants' second baseman, gave it to Everett Scott in the belly and knocked him out. Well, we had a meeting that night and planned to give the Giants the same kind of treatment from there in. We even chose Giants we were to "take care of" individually. But Barrow heard of it and went to see McGraw that night. He said to him, "Your boys have been playing pretty rough, John, and my lads are very sore about it. If that's the way you want it I think we have bigger and stronger guys on our club than Doyle, Fletcher, Kauff and Youngs. I'm not asking you to call it off, but if the Giants play the same way tomorrow some players are going to get pretty badly messed up, and I am laying odds you'll have more injured players than I'll have when the battle is over." Ed had a way of saying things that made you believe him.

The Giants were as meek as a college team next day, and Barrow also kept us in check.

Barrow still hadn't decided whether he intended to use me as a pitcher or an outfielder. The Red Sox had all of their service players back that year, a fact which might have put me back in the box. But Frazee was beginning to sell players to New York. He sold Duffy Lewis, Ernie Shore and Dutch Leonard to the rich Colonels of the Yankees. Leonard balked at signing with the Yanks because Jake Ruppert wouldn't put his salary in the bank in advance. So before Dutch pitched a game for New York, Ruppert sold him to Detroit.

The sales opened a gap in our left-field position but Barrow told me he still wanted me to take my regular turn. We opened in New York that year and I pitched a shutout against the Yankees in the Polo Grounds. As I got it later, Frazee was all for keeping me on the pitching staff. He used to call Barrow "Simon"—as in Simon Legree—and often at this period of my playing life would say, "Simon, you'll ruin that big boy as a pitcher before you know it."

In the first month of the season I took my regular turn every four days and played in most of the others in the outfield. It was rough. So one day I said to Barrow, "Manager, I don't think I can keep playing the outfield when I am not pitching. It tires me out too much."

Barrow grinned and said, "If you'd cut out your carousing and night life you wouldn't tire so quickly." I thought that was his final answer, but he began studying me more carefully, and then one day, several weeks after my beef, he put it up to me. He took me aside in the clubhouse and said, "Babe, what do you really want to do, pitch or play the outfield?"

"Well, I certainly like to hit," I started. That's as far as Barrow let me go.

"If you love to hit that much I'll just have to keep you in the game every day," he said. And though I still pitched in enough games to win eight and lose five that season, I began to devote most of my thoughts to hitting and mastering the outfield, and less to pitching.

As early as April I began to hit home runs, taking up where I had left off when I hit the 11 in 1918. The American League record at the time was 16 by "Socks" Seybold of the 1902 Athletics, and the recognized Major League record was 25 by Buck Freeman of the 1899 Washington National League club.

As I began poking them out of the parks wherever the Red Sox played I passed Seybold's old record, and a lot of interest developed when I went after Buck Freeman's old mark. I took that in my stride and was ready to coast, but some statistician dug through the old box scores and came up with an earlier mark of 27 home runs hit by Ed Williamson of the Chicago White Stockings in 1884.

I was getting hotter and hotter, and on September 20th I tied Williamson's mark when I drove a long homer off Lefty Williams, the little White Sox southpaw, who later was tossed out of the game in the Black Sox scandal.

In appreciation of my success as a home-run hitter, the Père Marquette Council of the Knights of Columbus gave me a day at Fenway Park. The park was crowded as if for a World Series. They gave me a lot of gifts, including a diamond ring which I wear to this day. It still remains one of my proudest possessions and one of the most cherished of the many gifts which my fans have been kind enough to shower on me.

After the game, Johnny Drohan, the Boston baseball writer, asked me what Frazee had personally given me for packing the park.

"A cigar," I said, honestly enough. Everybody thought it was hilarious, except Frazee.

The season didn't have much longer to go because only 140 games were played in 1919. But before the curtain was rung down I got two more homers, winding up with 29, the next to last one off Bob Shawkey, who soon was to become my teammate on the Yankees.

Four of my 29 homers that season were with the bases filled, and one of my grand slams did a good turn for my former Red Sox associate, Tris Speaker. It actually knocked Lee Fohl right off the managerial bench in Cleveland. The Indians were ahead when Fohl sent Fritz Coumbe, a former Red Sox member, to the mound as a relief pitcher with the bases filled. I knocked the ball over the high right-field screen at Cleveland's old League Park, giving the Red Sox the ball game. Jim Dunn, the Cleveland owner, got so sore at Fohl's pitching strategy that he fired Lee and put Tris Speaker in charge of the team.

Despite my 29 home runs, the Red Sox slipped badly in 1919, falling from their proud position of World's Champions to sixth place. There were a lot of things wrong with that ball club. In mid-July Carl Mays walked out of a ball game in Comiskey Park, Chicago. Carl, who had been a big winner in 1917 and 1918, couldn't forgive errors that were made in back of him and he was sure that some of the players weren't trying hard enough when he pitched. Barrow sent one of the kid players to the clubhouse to tell Mays to forget it and to come back into the game. But Mays already was in the shower, and told the kid to go back and tell Barrow that he was going on a fishing trip.

We never saw Carl again in a Red Sox uniform. While he was on that fishing trip Frazee, at Barrow's insistence, sold him to the Yankees for $40,000 and a couple of pitchers, Bob McGraw and Allan Russell. That deal stirred up a fearful mess. Ban Johnson tried to restrain the Yankees from using Mays, but Ruppert and Huston went to court, got permission to pitch Carl, and soon the entire league was throwing lawbooks.

To add to Boston's problems, I was a headache, and continued to have my share of trouble with Ed Barrow. But looking back now at one instance I can see its funny side.

In 1919 Barrow engaged Dan Howley, later manager of the Reds and Browns, as Red Sox coach. One of his duties was to keep me out of trouble. It should have been a fulltime job, but Dan thought it would be easy.

"I'll take care of Babe if I have to put a ring through his nose and lead him wherever I go," I heard him tell Barrow. Barrow said "Harumph."

Dan never quite got that ring through my nose. Along with a few other strong-backed and weak-minded Red Sox, I began working harder at having fun than I worked on the field. Washington had a particularly bad effect on me.

Barrow rarely went to bed until he knew all of his players were in, but I figured I could outfox him. I sneaked into the hotel at 6 o'clock one morning and thought I had gotten away with it until I heard a thundering knock on the door. Ed had tipped an Irish porter at the hotel to call him the moment I came in. The light was on in the room but I didn't answer the knock. Howley had already bawled me out, but that didn't matter. In charged Ed, looking surprisingly mad for a man wearing a dressing gown and slippers. He found me lying in bed, the covers over me, and smoking my pipe.

It took him back a bit, but not much.

"What the hell are you doing smoking a pipe at this hour of the morning?"

I took a few more puffs and replied off-handedly, "Oh, I always smoke like that in the middle of the night. It's restful, and then I can go back to sleep again."

Suddenly Barrow lunged forward, yanked off the covers, and found me fully dressed. He looked at me with a face full of scorn.

"You're a fine citizen, Babe. Yes, I must say you are a very fine citizen."

He then stamped out, and after a bit my relief turned to anger. By the time I got to our clubhouse at the Washington ball park I was shaking. I think it was indignation. I walked over to where Ed was dressing for the game and bawled, "If you ever come into my room like that again, you so-and-so, I'll punch you right in the nose."

Barrow looked me in the eye and quietly said, "Call me that again, Babe." By that time I already appreciated I'd said something for which I was sorry. I did not repeat it. Barrow turned to the players who were dressing all around us.

"As soon as you fellows are dressed I want every man to leave this clubhouse. Ruth will stay here. Then we'll lock the door and see who is the better man. No man can call me that and get away with it."

Harry Hooper and Dave Shean came over to Ed. "Don't fight him, Ed," Hooper said. "It won't do anybody any good."

But Barrow still was raging.

"I've just got to have it out with that young man," he answered.

I finished dressing when the others did and looked Ed over. I was 24; he was 50. I left the clubhouse with the others. I had sense enough to realize that I couldn't win even if I beat him.

I was shagging flies in the outfield when Barrow

took his accustomed place on the bench. He didn't pay any attention to me. So I trotted in and asked, "Am I playing today?"

"No, you are not playing, and get out of that uniform," Ed boomed. "You're suspended until further notice."

The Red Sox won without me that day, and that put Barrow in a better mood. We left Washington and returned to Boston. On the train I felt pretty penitent. That's the way I was through a good part of my life. I would do a lot of daffy things and quickly be sore at myself for having done them. I approached the compartment occupied by Barrow and Larry Graver, the club secretary, and knocked. Barrow called out, "Who is it?"

"It's me, Babe. Will you talk to me?"

Barrow called out again, "Come in, Babe." And as I entered Graver stepped outside.

I sat down and wheezed, "I'm awfully sorry for what happened at the ball field today."

"You ought to be!"

I still was feeling low and said, "Ed, someday somebody is going to kill me."

Barrow looked at me more kindly and answered, "Nobody's going to kill you, if I can help it, Babe. But don't you know you can't go around calling people names like that?"

"Yes, I know; I shouldn't do it," I mumbled.

Barrow stood up and looked at me for quite a long time. "What makes you act that way, Babe?" he said. "What kind of raising did you have?"

Instinctively my thoughts went back to my early days on the Baltimore waterfront, between the helpful periods I spent at St. Mary's. I started to say something about those days, but I didn't know how to say it.

Barrow seemed to sense this. He mellowed suddenly. "I'm sorry, Babe," he said. "I know you had tough going as a kid. But don't you want to lead a decent life now and grow up to be a fine citizen?"

"Yes, Ed, I really want to do that," I said eagerly, and I meant it.

We next discussed my conduct in staying out late. He told me some of the pitfalls of players he had managed in the past. Then I made him a proposition.

"Listen, Manager, if I leave a note in your box when I come back every night and put the exact time on it, will it be all right with you?" I asked.

"Can I take your word?" he wanted to know.

"You bet you can," I said, and we shook hands on it.

I never had any further trouble with Barrow so long as I remained in Boston. I imagine my notes to him sounded pretty bushy. I would head them, "Dear Manager" or "Dear Eddie" and they'd read: "I got back at eleven-thirty," or "two minutes before midnight," and I'd sign them, "Babe."

During my last season in Boston I had one unhappy experience the effects of which have remained with me more or less through life. I came up with a very sore throat and our trainer tried to cure it. I guess the treatment was right out of that book, "Kill or Cure." He got a big swab of cloth, put a lot of nitrate of silver on it, and reached deep into my throat. I know physicians use nitrate of silver in treating a sore throat condition, but it never should be applied by one who is not a skilled doctor.

I started to strangle. Barrow, who was near by, heard my gurgling gasps and quickly saw I was in a bad way. He started to take me to a hospital but decided I needed immediate help so he rushed me to a drugstore near Fenway Park. I had another spasm in the drugstore, but the druggist succeeded in relieving my condition to some extent.

With that barrel chest of mine I've always had a powerful voice. But I believe my husky voice came mostly from the change that nitrate of silver treatment made in my throat.

Barrow fired the trainer on the spot, but it was a good week before I could swallow solid food with any degree of comfort.

I do not recommend this as the best way of becoming a basso.

7

Broadway—
And 54 Home Runs

After the 1919 season I went out to California to play some winter baseball in the Los Angeles area. At that time it was standard practice for major leaguers to pick up exhibition dollars during the off-season.

There were a number of players with big names out there with me. I particularly remember Buck Weaver, the White Sox third baseman. Weaver got himself all messed up in the unhappy Black Sox scandal which did not break until late in the 1920 season.

Fans were speculating as to whether my 29 home runs of 1919 were just a freak occurrence or whether I could beat it with the majors returning to a 154-game season in 1920. Many baseball men and sports writers doubted if I ever could surpass the mark and felt that with baseball players getting settled after the war, and pitching improving, I'd be lucky if I would ever again hit even 20. However, there were some who contended that I hit a longer ball than any of the home-run hitters before me, and that with my pitching cares behind me there was no telling how far I might go.

The New York Yankees apparently were among those who believed that my showing with the 1919 Red Sox was no freak. They bought me in one of baseball's most sensational deals early in January, 1920. The price paid by Ruppert and Huston was estimated at the time, and generally accepted, at

$125,000. Later, I learned the exact details. The flat sum was $100,000, but Colonel Ruppert personally loaned Frazee $350,000, and Frazee put up Fenway Park as security.

Every now and then I am amused to read that it was Barrow who bought me for the Yankees. That's nutty. I preceded Ed to New York by a year. In fact, Barrow did everything possible to prevent Frazee from going through with it and roared like a bull when Frazee told him of his intentions.

Ed's first knowledge of the deal came one cold day in Boston when Frazee called him by long distance from New York and asked him to meet him the next day at the old Knickerbocker Hotel in New York. Barrow later told me that he got a bad feeling in his bones almost immediately. Call it intuition or anything you want, but Barrow kept saying to himself, "I'll bet 'Frazz' is selling Babe Ruth on me."

When Barrow called on Frazee the club owner said, "You know why I sent for you, Simon?"

Ed realized his fears were then justified. He said, "I have a hunch, but tell me what's on your mind."

Without mincing words Frazee pulled it on him. "I'm going to trade Babe Ruth to the Yankees," he announced. "I know how you feel, Ed, but Ruppert has made me a wonderful offer," Frazee said. "Ruppert's loaning me $350,000. I need it badly, Ed. Joe Lannin is pressing me for notes I gave when I bought the club. You're right in getting sore at me, but I had to do it."

Barrow waited a long time before he spoke. "And what do I get for Babe?"

"A hundred thousand dollars, and I'll get you some players from the Yankees."

Barrow was still sore and shouted, "Don't you insult me again with the kind of players you got from the Yankees in the Mays deal. Make it a straight cash transaction. We'll all look like asses if we try to tell our fans it's a trade."

They let me in on the secret a few days in advance, but I don't think I really appreciated how big the story was until I saw the papers the day it broke.

A few days before the story broke Miller Huggins, the pint-sized manager of the Yankees, appeared at my hotel in Los Angeles. I wasn't in when he called and he was waiting for me in the lobby when I showed up at last.

"I want to see you, Babe," Hug said.

"He's here to tell me that I've been sold or traded to the Yankees," I said to myself as I led him to my room and we talked of other things.

I didn't know Huggins very well at the time. He had been a National League player and manager and came into the American League during the war season of 1918 when he succeeded my old Providence friend, Bill Donovan, as manager of the Yankees. I'd heard Miller had been a pretty good second baseman and lead-off man and wondered how such a little guy could ever have been a good ballplayer. He didn't seem strong enough to swing a bat, or live through a spiking job. But people said he was a smart little fellow and knew a lot about baseball. As we sat there in my room, talking about everything except what was in our minds, neither of us sensed what the next ten years would bring to us in the way of fame, fortune, good and bad times.

Finally he said it: "How would you like to play for the Yankees?"

I told him I liked Boston and always had been happy with the Red Sox, but if Frazee sent me to the Yankees I'd try to play as hard there as I ever did in Boston.

Huggins coughed. "We haven't put through the deal yet, but I want to know whether you will behave yourself if we do obtain your services for the New York club. I know you've been a pretty wild boy in Boston, Babe, and if you come to New York it's got to be strictly business." He was wagging a finger at me by this time. "There are many temptations in the big city for an outstanding baseball hero, and I am asking you whether you think you can measure up to it."

I was getting a little fed up with this sermon.

"I've already told you I'll play the best I can, for the Yankees or anybody else. But listen, if I go to New York I'll want a lot more dough than the $10,000 Frazee paid me last year."

"I'm coming to that," Huggins replied. "We know you've built yourself to the top. Colonel Ruppert is a generous man and if you promise to behave yourself when you come to us the Yankees will tear up your old Red Sox contract and make it $20,000."

Huggins, Ruppert and Huston are all dead now; but until the time they died I believe each of them took credit for initiating the deal which brought me to the Yankees. Little Hug claimed it was he who suggested me to the two Colonels. It was Ruppert's wealth which enabled him to make the big loan to Frazee which made the deal possible. But I have always believed the idea originally was Huston's.

Ruppert and Huston bought the Yankees in 1915 and spent a fortune trying to build them into a winner. Ruppert was restless but Huston was downright impatient over the failures of the Yankee clubs and I believe it was he who first got the inside on Frazee's financial condition.

The reporters always called Huston "Cap," and he liked to sit around with a crowd of baseball men and sports writers and drink beer. Frazee was one of his favorite drinking companions, and I believe that it was over a few glasses of beer that Huston first learned of Frazee's need and that if the amount was right he could obtain me for the Yankees.

As for my reaction over coming to the big town, at

first I was pleased, largely because it meant more money. Then I got the bad feeling we all have when we pull up our roots. My home, all my connections, affiliations and friends were in Boston. The town had been good to me. I knew New York principally as a place where the Red Sox played eleven games a year, where I had hit some home runs, won some shutouts, consumed beer and had a lot of fun. Of course, as the years rode on, New York got me, the same as it gets most people who settle there. Today it is my home, and whenever I leave I am always happy to get back. And when people think of me as a ballplayer, they think of me as a Yankee.

I joined the Yanks in Jacksonville, Fla., late in February, 1920. There was something in the air and it was exciting. The club had finished third in 1919, but we all felt we were headed upward. Most fans believe the term "Murderers Row" started with my association with the Yankees in 1920. Actually, Bob Ripley drew a cartoon calling them that the year before when he sketched a gang of big bruisers swinging clubs, labelling them "Roger Peckinpaugh, Wally Pipp, Frank Baker, Del Pratt and Ping Bodie." Bob captioned it: "Murderers Row." I simply joined the Row.

But I was big news and the New York newspapers sent 13 reporters to cover that Yankee training camp, more than had ever followed any other big team up to that time. Even the *Morning Telegraph*, a newspaper devoted largely to racing, blew itself to a reporter, Weed Dickinson. We drew some first-class sports writers, among them the brilliant Damon Runyon; Sid Mercer, who had just switched over to the American League after John McGraw repudiated an interview on him; Bill Hanna, a funny little grouch, but a guy who knew his baseball; Fred Lieb, Dave Walsh, Buck O'Neill and a number of others whose names I've forgotten.

My first roommate was Ping Bodie, the good-natured California Italian. Ping never wasted words. In fact, he wasted fewer words than I wasted nights sitting around our room. Somebody once asked him who he roomed with and Ping replied, "Ruth's trunk."

Fred Lieb and his wife occupied a room next to us, and Fred told me of an amusing experience in my early days with the club. Mrs. Lieb went down to the hotel clerk to have her room changed because the noise of the elevator prevented her from sleeping at night. The clerk explained that there wasn't an elevator anywhere near her room. The next night she listened again, and realized that what she heard was our snoring. She thought it was a duet, but I set her straight by telling her that Bodie could snore an opera from start to finish. Maybe that's why I let Ping room with my trunk.

I didn't get along too well with the New York reporters at the start. I suppose all eyes were on me, and I didn't get off to a good start in a long training series with the Brooklyn Dodgers, who also were training in Jacksonville. Brooklyn had a club which won the championship that year and Uncle Robbie had some fine pitchers: Jeff Pfeffer, Rube Marquard, Al Mamaux and Sherry Smith. They began curving the ball early, and all the Yankees had trouble connecting safely. I struck out two or three times a game and thought nothing much about it until I saw the New York papers.

I suppose I didn't appreciate it, but I was big news down there, and when papers got to Jacksonville with headlines like, "Babe Strikes Out with the Bases Filled," "Babe Fizzles in the Pinch," "Babe Falls Down Again," I got pretty sore.

"I'll pop a couple of those newspaper guys if they don't lay off of me," I groused one day after a bad game.

Carl Mays overheard it and said, "That kind of talk

won't get you anywhere, Babe. Those fellows will be only too glad to write something nice about you if you give them something nice to write about. Go out and clip a few homers and you won't have any reason to bellyache about your write-ups."

But I couldn't get on the track.

One day a loud-mouthed fan got on me and called me every kind of bum he could think of. I just wasn't in a mood to take it, after an hour or so. I jumped over the bleacher fence and climbed up the stands after him. He was a little squirt but he didn't run. Instead, he pulled a knife on me. It looked about a foot long. I paused for a moment, but before I had a chance to tackle him Colonel Huston jumped in between us. He had seen me go into the bleachers and had run across the field and jumped the bleacher rail to act as a peace officer. He didn't have much trouble keeping me from tangling with that knife.

I believe it was the very next day that I got going. Al Mamaux, a fast-ball pitcher, was throwing for the Dodgers and I really got hold of one. Though most of my long hits went to right field, this one was almost to dead center. Like the long ball which I hit off George Smith in Tampa the spring before, it wasn't a high drive but was still at its maximum height of 30 feet when it went over the center fielder's head and on to the deepest part of the field.

That clout was the spark I needed to touch me off. From then on I began hitting them regularly, both in Jacksonville and at the other points we visited in our training jaunt.

Shortly before we broke camp at Jacksonville we went down to Miami for, I guess, one of the wildest excursious ever made by a Big League ball club. We were scheduled for two games in Miami and one at Palm Beach. It was early in the Prohibition period and Miami was a hot harbor for the hooch-running business. The Cincinnati Reds trained there, and as

World's Champions I suppose they felt it their duty to entertain us New Yorkers in proper style. And those Yankees who didn't have pals on the Reds found plenty of entertainment when they were on their own.

The same went for "Cap" Huston and the reporters who went to a party at Bimini the night after our second game. Returning in the early hours of the morning one reporter didn't want to get off the launch. Another tried to give him a helping hand but got pulled into Biscayne Bay for his efforts.

Well, we had a lot of bleary eyes the next morning, and three guys had to assist Ping Bodie to the train. But at least Ping didn't fall in the ocean.

There was a beautiful setting for our game in Palm Beach. It was one of those fine March days, with blue skies and a warm sun, and a crowd filled the place in the hope of seeing me hit one. I did hit one—a palm tree. It grew in fair territory deep in the outfield. I guess my reflexes were a bit off that day. Anyway, I ran into the tree, chasing a ball in fielding practice and knocked myself cold. For a while it looked as if the Yanks had tied up $450,000 in a dead duck. But I regained consciousness finally, and Huggins gave me the rest of the day off.

We heard about that trip to Miami for years afterward, and as long as Ruppert lived the Yankees never returned there for another game.

I had to share the spotlight on the trip North. Damon Runyon bought an alligator. If my memory is correct, he called it "Alice." He bought it during our trip to Miami, and from there on gave daily reports on it which highlighted his stories in the old New York *American*. I went to him one day and said, "Hey, Damon, who are you covering on this trip, me or an alligator?"

"I can't keep writing about your lousy home runs every day," he said, feeding his monster.

"Alice" died suddenly while we were in Washington, our last stop before returning to New York, and you would have thought Damon had lost his best friend. But I got back in his column.

We opened the 1920 season in Philadelphia. Thousands of New York fans went over to Philly to see us get started, but I let them down with a poor opening day. The next afternoon was better. A Philadelphia hatmaker presented me with a brown derby at home plate before the game. I clapped it on my noggin and everything suddenly went brown. It was so big it came down over my eyes and ears.

The crowd gave me a friendly hand when I groped my way to the dugout, wearing the derby. Maybe it was as lucky as Al Smith's. I don't know. But I got hits to all corners of Shibe Park that day, and kept hitting.

I was soon back in my old home-run stride of 1919, and I kept plugging in the hope of stepping up the pace. The Polo Grounds, where the Yanks of that day played their 77 home games, was just right for me. If I had spent my best playing years at that ball park I'm sure I eventually would have hit more than my record total of 60. There is, of course, no way of saying how many I would have hit—though it has been suggested that I might have gotten 75 or even 100.

In batting practice at the Polo Grounds I sometimes used to clown around and hit one-handed home runs into the lower right-field stands, something like Brother Matthias used to do with a fungo bat at St. Mary's, when I was his bug-eyed audience.

By midseason I matched the 29 of 1919, and after that every additional home run was a new record. People found it hard to believe, when I finally hit 54 that year, as the fans of today would react to—say—some kid who hit 200. I finished the 1920 season with a batting average of .376 for my first year as a Yank. I got 36 doubles and nine triples in addition to my homers, scored 156 runs, and drove in 137. I don't think

I'm bragging when I say I made the country home run conscious.

The Yankees had never won a pennant prior to my coming to New York, but in 1920 we came close, and should have copped our first one. We were in a season-long race with the Indians and White Sox which lasted right down to the final week of play. Eventually, the Indians won their only pennant, beating out the White Sox by two games and us by three. We lost the flag in our last Western trip after we seemed to have it sewed up.

There was a real tragedy at the Polo Grounds in August, when Carl Mays pitched a ball which struck Ray Chapman, the Cleveland shortstop, under the left ear. The blow cracked poor Ray's skull and he died the next night. It produced a lot of bad feeling between our two clubs, and Mays, who was our leading pitcher, did not accompany us on our last trip to Cleveland. Even without Mays we won our final series in Cleveland and took the lead by two points. We held it in Detroit but we met our Waterloo in Chicago.

Colonel Ruppert had a close pal, a lame chap by the name of Billy Fleischman, whose name used to appear on the club's stationery as Assistant to the President. He was a nice old fellow, but a jinx if I ever saw one. Every time he joined us on the road we fell to pieces.

When we walked into our hotel in Chicago, for the year's most important series, the first guy we saw was Fleischman. He loved to see us play and couldn't stay away. "Holy cow," I said, "there's that guy Fleischman again to put the whammy on us!"

Fleischman came through again. We lost three straight to the White Sox and then Shocker beat us for the only time we lost four straight all year. We dived from first place to third in nothing flat.

I still can see "Cap" Huston in the dining room at the Cooper-Carlton Hotel in Chicago during that series. He sat at a large table, big enough for all the New York writers, and our tables were near by. After we had lost our first two to the White Sox Huston banged his big fist on the table one night and yelled so loud that he could be heard all over the dining room.

"This race is not over!" he shouted dramatically. "Remember what Commodore Perry said at Lake Erie. Don't give up the ship until your trunks hit the water."

Poor Hug! He had a hell of a time during the final phase of that trip. Huston never was for him and felt that Ban Johnson and others had moved Hug into the manager's spot while Huston was fighting in France. Huston's candidate for the job after Bill Donovan was let out had been Wilbert Robinson, the roly-poly manager from Brooklyn.

Huston was most critical of Huggins' use of pitchers in that final series, not only to the sports writers, but also to the ballplayers, and it didn't help Miller hold the players' respect. He was a little guy physically, and many of us, including myself, took advantage of him. Hug then made things worse when he told Huston, after we lost the opener in Chicago, "I still think we can finish second, Cap."

"Who the hell wants to finish second!" stormed Huston and walked away.

To make matters still worse, a few days after Chicago kicked us out of the race, the Black Sox scandal broke and eight of their leading players were booted out of baseball. Had that scandal broken a week before we could easily have beaten the second-stringers that Kid Gleason was forced to put into the game and we would have won our first pennant in 1920 instead of 1921.

There's something about a home run. Our long knocks and the race we made of it up to the last minute, enabled the Yanks that year to draw the unheard-of attendance of 1,289,422 at the Polo Grounds, which then had a capacity of only 33,000. That stood as the American League record until the Yankees beat it themselves in 1946 by going over two million.

We also were a wonderful draw on the road. No matter where we went the fans swarmed out to see "Baby Ruth," as some called me, hit home runs. I recall one series we played in St. Louis. Fred Lieb brought three cowboys into the locker room to shake hands with me. They told me they had ridden three days to a little railroad station in Wyoming to flag a train for St. Louis, and now having seen a couple of games, they were heading home to their ranch. They wore chaps and spurs and cowboy hats, and as they left one of them said, "Baby Ruth, I'd have ridden on horseback all the way to St. Louis to see you hit them home runs."

Baseball was rocked by the scandal that followed the disclosure late in the 1920 season that the 1919 Reds–White Sox World Series had been fixed. To me, it was like hearing that my Church had sold out. No matter what grievances some of those White Sox players had against Owner Charley Comiskey, I couldn't comprehend how any Big League players could defraud not only the millions of fans all over the country, but millions of kids, by throwing the biggest sporting event of the year.

The men who ran the game picked Judge Kenesaw Landis to run baseball the following winter, and the old Judge did a fine job as the first Commissioner. It has been said that Landis saved the game from ruin after the Black Sox scandal. Others say that I had a lot to do with the game's salvation. The important thing is that baseball snapped back. If my home-run hitting in 1920 established a new era in baseball, helped the fans of the nation, young and old, forget the past and the terrible fact that they had been sold out, that's all the epitaph I want.

The first attempt to write my life was made that season by Westbrook Pegler. Pegler was working then for a news syndicate and it sent him with the Yankees on a Western trip to get the low-down. Well, I was pretty hard to run down at that stage of my career. My legs were better then. There were so many things to do and places to go after I finished my job at the ball park that every time Peg tried to get me to sit down with him I'd remember a date and say, "I'll see you tomorrow." He chased me from Cleveland to Detroit to Chicago, and finally caught up with me in church one Sunday morning in St. Louis.

In 1920 I also had my first experience with motion pictures. Several sharp fellows smoked me up about how they were going to make me a millionaire with a picture starring me. The film was called "The Babe Comes Home," and the titles were written, I believe, by Bugs Baer. A story about a farm kid who crashed into the big leagues with a lot of home runs and fell for a blonde. I was to get $50,000 and the "rest" later when the movie fans of the country flocked to their neighborhood theaters to see me on the screen. I did get $15,000 and a check for $35,000. They told me not to deposit it for a week. But when I did put it in my bank it bounced and bounced and bounced.

They shot the picture across the river from New York at Fort Lee, N. J. It was ground out in the mornings before I reported to the Polo Grounds. For about a week I missed batting practice and showed up at the park with make-up on my face. Schang, Bob Meusel and Wardie kidded the pants off me, and Hug was so sore he sizzled.

"What are you, a movie actor or a ball player?" he brayed at me. I didn't have the answer just then. I hadn't seen the picture.

They first showed the picture at the old Madison

Square Garden. They gave it a lot of cheap ballyhoo but it played to empty seats. There never was a movie quite like "The Babe Comes Home."

Thank God.

8

Our Yankees Win a Pennant

There were a lot of people in 1920 who didn't think I'd ever again approach my 29 homers of 1919. It was the same in 1921. They thought my 54 of 1920 was such an unheard-of accomplishment that no one again could ever push it up that high.

I not only increased my 1921 homer production to 59, but my 1921 batting average of .378, 177 runs scored and 170 runs driven in, helped to drive the Yanks to their first pennant. Incidentally, that 177 runs scored still remains the American League record.

By 1921 we had quite a Boston colony on the Yankees. In fact, it began to look more and more like the old Red Sox. Duffy Lewis, Ernie Shore and Carl Mays preceded me to the Yankees, but shortly before the 1921 season Ruppert and Huston swung another deal whereby they obtained catcher Wallie Schang, pitchers Waite Hoyt and Harry Harper, and my old friend of the box score, Mike McNally.

The Yankees gave up another chunk of money, but also sent Boston some pretty good players, including "Muddy" Ruel, the little catcher who now coaches Cleveland, Del Pratt and Sammy Vick. Vick preceded me in right field for New York, and they say he had even a better appetite than I had at that time—which made him a glutton. Huggins later said that getting rid of Ruel was his biggest mistake as a Big League manager because the little receiver later developed into one of the great catchers in the game. But we got a sweet catcher in Schang and another 20-game winner in Waite Hoyt. Waite and I were pals in Boston but much closer in New York. Our lockers were next to each other. We used to scrap and ride each other, and then be friends, go out on the town together, get in another fight and make up again. I never met a finer competitor than Hoyt.

But about the biggest Yankee-Red Sox deal of that time saw Ed Barrow come to us, to give the proper balance to our business office. Ed stopped the long-winded arguments between Ruppert and Huston and helped protect Miller Huggins from both Huston and some of the more independent ballplayers, including myself.

Ed's first act of office was to move our spring training camp from Jacksonville to Shreveport. I had picked up some free-living friends in Jacksonville, but Shreveport really opened my eyes. There was an oil boom on there at the time and the town was wide open, with some of the toughest and freest-spending people I ever met.

Ray Kelly, now the dignified sports editor of *The New York Times,* was a kid baseball writer with us that year. He was fresh out of Fordham and just about the best-eating newspaperman I ever saw. I was interested in such things. Ray was with the old *Tribune* at that time, and the club roomed him with a young reporter from the *Post,* Bob Kelley, who had been gassed during the first World War and was given to fainting spells, particularly on the tennis court. We called Ray, "Carniverous Kelly" and Bob, "Collapsible Kelley."

I now had a body of 220 pounds and it took a lot of food to feed it. Sid Mercer and some of the other writers tried to plot up an eating contest between me and "Carniverous Kelly." I was willing to take on anybody, including a hungry cannibal, but Hug heard about it and nixed the idea.

The writers pulled another great gag on "Carniverous Kelly" that spring. Hoyt and I and some of the other ballplayers were in on it. Kelly had been in the same graduating class at Fordham with Frankie Frisch and was a great booster of the Fordham Flash. So some of the ribbers sent Kelly a fake telegram signed "Ed Barrow," which read, "THIS IS TO TELL YOU THAT THE YANKEES ALSO HAVE A SECOND BASEMAN, AARON WARD. INASMUCH AS YOU ARE EATING US OUT OF HOUSE AND HOME, FORGET ABOUT FRISCH AND WRITE SOMETHING ABOUT WARD."

Every time we used to pass Kelly after that we'd yell, "Write something about Ward for a change, will you?"

Brooklyn trained at New Orleans that spring and we met them in a grapefruit league game at Alexandria. I got hold of a ball there on the fat part of my bat and drove it over the right-field fence. It was still sailing when the reporters in the press box last saw it. I forgot it, like most of the others. But another fellow didn't.

A year later the train in which the Giants were heading North stopped in Alexandria, La., for five or ten minutes to drink some water and a big Negro fellow got on board mumbling, "Which one of you is Babe Ruth?" He first went into the car occupied by the Giant players, and as there always is a lot of kidding on a ball club they told him I was in the last car, the one occupied by the New York writers. The reporters tried to explain to the guy that I was with the New York Yankees and that this was a trainload of Giants. But the fellow wouldn't listen.

"I know this is the New York club, that Babe Ruth plays on the New York club, and you're trying to hide him from me," he insisted.

In the meantime he was waving a piece of paper in his paw. So one of the writers, sensing a story, asked, "What do you want to see Ruth so badly about?"

"I want to give him this bill," the colored man said.

The writer asked him how I happened to owe him money and the bloke answered, "When Babe Ruth was here a year ago he hit one of the damndest home runs that anybody ever did see. It went far over the right-field fence, way over the high trees in back of the ball park, and never stopped until it went through the window of my house, three blocks away. It cost me $2.75 to put in three new panes of glass, and he's gotta pay for it."

I got hot during the spring games in 1921 and stayed hot after the American League opened. I hit 59 home runs that year and at least half of them were smacked off bad balls, pitches I had to reach for. Nobody gave me a good ball to hit. But if they were anywhere near the plate I took a cut at them.

Up until this period no one had ever hit a home run into the old center-field wooden bleachers at the Polo Grounds. Joe Jackson, and several others, including myself, had knocked a few into the seats in right center. I began taking aim at the more distant seats. Detroit came to town for a midseason series and decided to pitch to me. I hit two into the center-field seats on consecutive days. Both shots had to carry more than 400 feet and still have height at the end, because the bleachers stood about 20 feet off the ground. One of these homers was made off George Dauss.

George sure was my "cousin." I drove him nuts. No matter where he'd pitch the ball—high, low, inside or outside—I was able to belt it. Long hits off him always gave me a lot of fun. Ty Cobb was manager of the Tigers by that time and every long hit I made was a personal insult to him. He'd run in from center field to tell the pitcher what to throw to me, but that would only make me more determined to slug the ball.

I had seen Chapman killed and I had a bad feeling in those days that I might kill a pitcher with a line drive. I believe the one I came closest to knocking dead was Howard Ehmke, Cobb's long, lanky right-hander. Ehmke will vouch for that. One day I leaned against one of his pitches and drove it back like a shot—right at his head. It missed him by a fraction of an inch. Howard was white as a sheet and still quaking when he got up. So was I.

Another time I hit one through the legs of Hod Lisenbee, the Washington pitcher, and it cleared the head of the Washington center fielder. I used to pray that I'd never contribute to another fatal baseball injury.

On the lighter side, that season I hit what has been called the highest infield fly that ever took off from a big leaguer's bat. We still were playing morning and afternoon games on holidays, and this was the morning end of a Fourth of July game with the Athletics at the Polo Grounds. I don't know exactly how I hit that ball, but it went almost straight up in the air and kept going until it was more than twice the height of the Polo Grounds' roof. It finally looked like a pea up there against the morning sky.

As I ran around to second, Jimmy Dykes, who was then playing second base for Connie Mack, staggered around the infield trying to get under it. He finally did get his fingertips on the ball at the edge of the infield, but he couldn't hold it. When he returned to the bench Connie Mack said, "Good boy, Jimmy; you didn't let it hit you on the head."

I thought for sure they would score a ball hit that high as a two-bagger, and I was considerably annoyed when I saw next morning's paper and found out that it had been scored as an error for Dykes.

I knew that Fred Lieb was the official scorer up to that time, and when I saw him the next time I barked, "What do you have to do in this league to get a base hit?"

He explained to me that he hadn't scored the play, as George Daley, then of the *Morning World,* was starting his half of the season as scorer on the Fourth of July, and that he had called the play. I thought Fred was trying to put me off, though I later learned he had told the truth and that Daley actually had deprived me of this hit. But for the next couple of weeks every time I saw Lieb I continued to yell at him that same question, "What do you have to do in this league to get a base hit?" Finally, on a train to St. Louis, he yelled back to me, "Hit them out of the infield." That stopped me.

We had a great two-team race that season with the Cleveland Indians, the 1920 World's Champions. Neither team ever got more than a game or two ahead.

By the time Cleveland came to New York for its final series in late September we led by two percentage points. It was a four-game series, and the team that took three out of four was almost certain to win the flag. We took the first one. Waite Hoyt won the opener by a score of 4 to 2. They then made us look bad in the second game, when Uhle shut us out 9 to 0.

Everybody in New York tried to crowd his way into the Polo Grounds on Sunday for the third game. This time we really put the wood to Speaker's pitchers and gave that crowd something to shout about, pulverizing a half dozen of Cleveland's pitchers by a score of 21 to 7.

By the fourth game both managers had pretty well used up their pitching staffs and Hug didn't know whom to pitch for us. I guess this probably was the only time in baseball that a manager permitted his pitching staff to select the pitcher for a vital game. Hug called a meeting of the whole staff and asked the boys to help him choose the right pitcher. He said he could start Jack Quinn, who had beaten the Indians in Cleveland earlier in the month, or come back with Hoyt, who had won the first game of the series. The staff finally voted to start Quinn, with Hoyt in the bull pen.

What followed was one of the wildest games I ever was in, and I am happy to remember I swung the big club that finally gave us an 8 to 7 victory. I hit two homers, a double, and drove in four runs. I had to, because George Burns, the Cleveland first baseman also drove in four with a triple and three singles.

The staff picked Quinn but it wasn't a good selection. The Indians knocked him out by scoring three runs in the first before he could get a man out. Hoyt then came in and did pretty well until the eighth, when he also got his bumps, and Carl Mays finished.

I'll never forget the ninth inning. It was in the early fall and the days were getting shorter. By the ninth it was almost as dark as in the fourteenth inning of my 1916 World Series victory in Boston. Cleveland had the tying run on second, with two out. Steve O'Neill, the present Tiger manager, and then Cleveland's catcher, was at bat. He was really itching to bust one. Mays saw this and threw one right into the dirt and Steve struck out.

That last inning had its amusing side. Jake Ruppert, our boss, just couldn't take it. He had been watching the game from the downstairs' press stand, which was then directly behind the home plate. But in the ninth inning the tension became too much for him. He and his friend Billy Fleischman ran out of the press box and hid under the grandstand until the inning was over. It wasn't until he heard the shout of the crowd when O'Neill struck out that he knew we had won this important ball game.

Winning that vital game practically assured us of the pennant, though Urban Shocker, the big spitball pitcher of the Browns, shut us out next day, and we didn't clinch the pennant until the final Saturday of the season, when we walloped the Athletics.

Since then the Yankees have won so many pennants

the fans almost have lost track of them. But that first flag was like the first of 15 children. It was wonderful! New York had been waiting 18 years for its first American League pennant and the town went wild, especially as the Giants had won that season in the National League.

Ruppert was a quieter kind of fellow than Huston, but he was supremely happy. "Cap" Huston came into the clubhouse with his black derby. "You big so-and-so," he said to me; "you surely are worth every nickle we put into you."

Poor little Hug was so happy his eyes were filled with tears. He had a tough team to manage. I was no angel and gave him plenty of sleepless nights. Carl Mays wasn't the easiest guy to handle, and Waite Hoyt was another hotheaded kid with his own ideas about pitching and living.

Once after Huggins ordered Waite to walk a hitter they had an argument on the bench and the "Schoolboy," as we called Hoyt, tried to take a poke at the little manager. It might have been a nasty situation if another player hadn't grabbed Waite's arm.

Bob Meusel was another guy who was in and out of Huggins' doghouse. But after we clinched the pennant we were so happy that everything was forgiven and forgotten.

As I just said, McGraw won in the other league, and all of old New York was pretty well het up over the first subway World Series. We then were playing for five games out of nine with the players sharing in the first five games.

Up until the time I came to New York it was pretty much of a National League town. The Giants had been the pennant winners, and the Yankees, known as the Highlanders in their early days, were always the poor relations. But the home-run hitting of the Yankees changed all that and we easily outdrew them in 1920 and 1921.

John McGraw didn't like that for a cent. He was proud of the past records and prestige of the Giants and his own position as the top man of New York baseball. It was evident then that the 1921 World Series would be for blood. As I say, we had outdrawn the Giants, and if we could defeat them in the Series we'd have McGraw where he decidedly was playing second fiddle.

After our grand start in the 1921 World Series, winning two shutout games by 3 to 0 scores—pitched by Carl Mays and Waite Hoyt—we thought we were in. We even scored four runs in the third game before the Giants scored their first run of the Series. But after getting away to a start like that we finally finished on the wrong end, losing five games out of eight.

It still burns me up, for I accidentally played a part in the loss. I developed an abscess on my left elbow a few days before the Series. I played in the first five games under difficulties, and even though I hit .313, knocked out my first World Series home run, and batted in four runs, I should have done more. I had to sit on the bench for the sixth, seventh and eighth games, though I made one pinch-hitting appearance in the last contest.

Anybody who knows how I loved to play baseball and liked to hit can imagine how I felt, sitting out those games when my bat was needed so badly in the Yankee line-up. This was especially true of the seventh and eighth games when Mays and Hoyt lost heartbreakers by scores of 2 to 1 and 1 to 0.

Chick Fewster, a Baltimore boy like myself, filled in for me and hit a home run in the sixth game. But it wasn't enough, and I couldn't do anything about it.

There was an especially unpleasant experience before the eighth game which still rankles after all these years. It was the only time I ever was accused of soldiering or letting down my team in a big series.

For some reason I never could learn, Joe Vila, then

sports editor of the New York *Sun,* never liked me, and now he printed a column in which he criticized me for sitting out the sixth and seventh games. There were some references in his story to my "alleged injury," and the general slant of the column was that I was happy to have the pressure off me.

I blew my top and decided to show him my arm. The lancing job on it had left some of the bone exposed. I went after him.

Joe was a big man, but considerably older than I. I found him in the front row of the press stand. The screen was between us but as I approached him with fire in my eyes he picked up his typewriter to defend himself as though he expected me to punch my way right through the screen. I called him something and added, "You're accusing me of not having any guts. Now, if *you* have any, print a picture of my arm with this hole in it and let your readers see my side of it." The picture was never printed.

We lost the final game of the 1921 Series when Roger Peckinpaugh, our shortstop and captain, fumbled a ball in the first inning which let in the only Giant run. The game wound up in a most spectacular double play. We had Ward on first base, with one out, and Frank Baker at bat. We badly needed that run to tie up the game, and if we could have won the game the Series would have been knotted at four games apiece.

Baker shot one toward right field that we all thought was a hit but Johnny Rawlings, the Giants' second baseman, knocked it down on the grass and threw Baker out while on his knees.

In the meantime, Ward tried to go to third base. Rawlings' throw to first baseman George Kelly wasn't too good, but George grabbed the ball and, turning quickly, pegged the ball across the diamond to Frisch at third. Frisch, Ward and the ball all came to the bag together, but Frankie tagged Ward just as he was sliding into the bag, and we were dead ducks. You won't see one play like that in ten years.

I got into one of the big jams of my life immediately after the Series. Shortly after Landis came in he put through a new rule prohibiting players on championship clubs to barnstorm after the World Series. I resented that rule and still think it was unfair. In the past I had picked up considerable loose change in post-season exhibition games, and, rule or no rule, I decided to continue.

A promoter engaged about half a dozen of us to go on a barnstorming trip immediately after the Series. The club was to be built around Bob Meusel, Carl Mays, Wallie Schang and myself. We also had a couple of second-string pitchers, Billy Piercey and Tom Sheehan, later a Minor League manager and one of the managers of the Hotel Stevens in Chicago. And the rest of the club was to be made up of New York semi-pros.

Landis naturally got wind of our plans in a hurry. He asked me to telephone him, and I called him up the night after we lost the last game. He came right to the point.

"Babe, you'd better not make that trip," the old man warned me. "If you do, there will be a lot of consequences."

Huston got the news later that night that Landis was on the warpath after me and made a last-minute effort to try to stop us. But I told him I had made an agreement with that promoter to make this trip, and I was going through with it.

Knowing there was going to be hell to pay for anybody who made the trip, Schang and Mays decided at the last moment not to go. But Meusel, Piercey, Sheehan and myself took a midnight train for Buffalo. We played that day and two more days.

It was reported that the trip then was abandoned because of lack of interest, but what really happened was that Huston paid off the promoters and the players involved to get them to call off the trip.

I took most of the rap. In his column in the Sun, Joe Vila asked, "If Babe couldn't play in the World Series how can he play an exhibition in Buffalo?" Nobody would listen to my explanation. The truth of the matter was I usually healed quickly. The abscess had been lanced, and after three days I again could swing a bat.

Maybe we were screwy. Maybe we were crusaders for the rights of ballplayers. But Landis gave us the full works. Our World Series shares were withheld from us, and Meusel, Piercey and I were suspended until May 20, 1922, which meant the first 39 days of the 1922 season.

The season of 1921 was also the one in which I acquired my manager, Christy Walsh, who made a lot of money for me as I did for him. But I'll always be grateful for what Christy did for me. Christy is a persistent guy who just won't take no for an answer. In fact, that's how he became my manager.

When I knocked out those 54 homers in 1920 I got all kinds of outside offers such as the movie I've already told about. People wanted me to endorse everything from suspenders to wallpaper. My first wife, Helen, and I tried to sift through them and pick out the best ones. We never knew what was sound or wildcat.

I always liked people and never was a difficult guy to see. But by 1921 they had me plain nuts. They'd camp on the doorstep of the apartment house in which I then lived in Washington Heights, back of the Polo Grounds, and I used to have to sneak in through the janitor's entrance to get to my own apartment. I'd put in a private, unlisted phone and a couple of weeks later all kinds of strangers would have my number and want to argue baseball with me and I'd have to change it again. If I had talked to everyone who propositioned me I'd never have had any time to play ball or eat or sleep.

That was the situation when Walsh tried to contact me. I shooed him away at the ball park, from my apartment door and when he tried to waylay me on the street. But Christy was not easily discouraged, and he was a strategist besides. He unearthed a neighborhood home-brew dealer I used to patronize and darned if he didn't get into my apartment as a delivery boy.

I didn't realize anything was wrong with the "delivery boy" until he refused to take any money and asked me how much a New York paper was paying me for a piece that was being ghosted for me—in which I told what kind of a pitch I had hit for a home run.

"Five bucks an article," I said. "Why?"

"I'll get you $500 for any article you write," he told me. Then he broke down and told me who he was, how he had tracked me down, and what he could do for me. I signed up then and there, and I'm more grateful today than I was at that time.

Christy took charge of all my outside earnings. I'd growl at him now and then, and occasionally would want to wring his neck when he'd put my money where I couldn't reach it, for I was always a fellow who could spend it faster than I could make it. During my first year under Christy's management my newspaper earnings alone jumped from less than $500 to $15,000. And that was only one sideline he improved for me.

About that same time I decided I should not stay at the same hotels as the rest of the club, because I usually had a lot of fair-weather friends (who seemed good, at the time) on my neck. In Washington, for instance, the Yanks stayed in $3 rooms at the Wardman Park. But not Babe, the Boy Spender. I stopped at the Raleigh, in a $100-a-day suite.

And travel with the Yanks on short hops? Nothing

doing! I had long since forgotten the day when I bought a bicycle with my first pay check from the Orioles and rode it around as proudly as any Indian prince ever rode a jewel-studded elephant.

But now, with the Yanks, I had a long, low Packard roadster, painted a fire-engine red, and there wasn't any greater thrill in life for me than stepping on that baby's gas. During the 1921 season, I nearly killed myself and four others, in that car. We had played the final game of a series with Washington and I had had a good day. Hug didn't like the idea, but I told him I'd drive my car to Philadelphia, for the next day's game, and get there before the train.

I had Helen along with me, our coach Charley O'Leary and a couple of players. Just outside of Kennett Square, Pa.—Herb Pennock's home town—I hit a turn too fast and we started to skid. Finally we turned over and rolled like a ball, with bodies flying out of the car in every direction.

For some reason which I can never understand if I live to be a hundred, none of us was hurt. The car was completely wrecked. I just left it there and bought a new one. (Incidentally, I hit a home run against the Athletics the next day despite the fact that one newspaper had come out with a big headline story announcing my death.)

Christy, as I said, helped keep me out of such scrapes, and later my second wife, Claire, and my attorney, Melvyn Gordon Lowenstein, gave me the best business advice an easy-come, easy-go guy ever had.

The trust funds and annuities they made me set up turned out to be godsends to me in later years, when, for reasons I'll speak of later, baseball had no place for me.

I don't mean to say that Christy completely reformed me. I kicked up a lot of dust even after I met him. But he helped. So did Jimmy Walker, as I'll tell you later. So did my realization that I meant something to American kids. And so did Brother Matthias. The club called him a couple of times to "talk" to me. I guess I didn't give him much chance, I was so glad to see him. Once, in a burst of gratitude, when I got sentimental about what he had done for me as a kid, I presented Brother Matthias with a Cadillac. He stalled it on some train tracks near St. Mary's not long after that, and a freight came along and smacked it lopsided. So I gave him another one.

I'd have bought him one every week, if he hadn't put a stop to it.

But I'm getting ahead of my story.

9

I Flop,
But We Win Again

I had such a bad season in 1922 I felt that I wasn't earning my money, which gives you an idea of how bad it was. I started bad that season and ended worse—hitting only .118 in the World Series against the Giants, which McGraw's club won easily. The best we could do was tie the second game.

I became the highest paid man in baseball that year, when I signed a five-year contract worth more than a quarter of a million dollars.

I had been paid $20,000 for my first season with the Yankees, and in 1921 they upped it to $30,000, though they were obliged to pay me only $20,000.

However, I was drawing more and more people all the time, at home and abroad, and I felt I deserved another raise in 1922. So I put the question to Huston, and he told me to get in shape while he talked it over with Ruppert.

Getting in shape wasn't easy. Thanks to the kind of life I was leading, a lot of meat had formed on the hard skinny frame I had brought into the majors. I went to Hot Springs, Ark., to boil out and try to pare myself down to what I figured was my best playing weight, 220 pounds.

I had company at Hot Springs. The New York *News* had assigned little Marshall Hunt to follow me wherever I went. He confined his writing to stories about me. To be sure I wouldn't get out of his sight, he even arranged to use the next tub to mine in the baths.

Huston, with his iron hat and belly something like mine, came down a few days after I arrived. He took the tub on the other side of mine and we talked business while we lost weight.

I think his first offer was $40,000 for five years. I turned it down, and kept turning down subsequent offers until he got up to $50,000. There we got stalled. I wanted $52,000 and when he raised cain, and asked me why, the only thing I could think of saying was, "I just want to make a thousand dollars a week, that's all."

Finally, we flipped a coin for it. I had played a lot of poker for stiff stakes, but this was something new. I won the toss. It was worth $10,000 over the span of the contract.

As soon as I signed the contract, Huston decided he could get a lecture off his chest.

"Babe," he said, "you've done a lot for our club. But you've also been an awful headache to me, and Jake and Hug. You've got to keep out of scrapes. We're investing a lot of money in you, and the only way you can earn it is by staying in shape. You've got to get away from those bright lights and settle down."

I had to laugh, for nobody liked bright lights, or hated settling down, more than Huston. But after reminding him of that, I promised him that I'd try to do better.

Huston brought along a bonus for me: he had persuaded Ruppert and Huggins to make me captain of the Yankees, despite the fact that I had a suspension hanging over me from the previous fall's barnstorming mess. I was to succeed Roger Peckinpaugh as captain.

Peck was traded away in another one of those Yankee-Frazee transactions during the winter. It was a rather involved deal, and we came up with three more of the Red Sox stars: pitchers Sam Jones and Joe Bush, and their sweet-fielding shortstop, Everett Scott. In addition to Peck, the Colonels sent a big check to Boston, plus three pitchers: Jack Quinn, Rip Collins and Bill Piercey. But Peck didn't stay in Boston. In another deal he went to the Athletics for Joe Dugan, after which he bounced to Washington in still another deal.

I was happy to get that captaincy. A quarter of a century ago a captain meant a lot more on a ball club than he does today. In some respects he was an assistant manager. He not only carried out the manager's orders on the field, but had his own responsibilities in the team's play. It made me feel good to think that the club had put a little responsibility on my shoulders.

We trained that year at New Orleans, always a gay spot, but especially so during Prohibition. And we were natural roof-raisers.

Despite the fact that Judge Landis had suspended Bob Meusel and myself for the first 39 days of the 1922 season, Ruppert, Huston and Huggins insisted we train as faithfully as if we were to be in our opening line-up. The Colonels thought that Judge Landis would relent. They moved heaven and earth to try to make him change his decision, or at least commute our sentences to about two weeks.

The New York fans also joined in the crusade. One newspaper got up a petition which was signed by 10,000 fans and sent it to the Commissioner. But the old Judge was about as easy to budge as an Alp.

During the winter the Colonels and their lawyer tried to point out to Landis that by suspending me he really was punishing the Yankee ball club and the other clubs of the American League, and therefore acting in restraint of trade.

In a final appeal for clemency, Ruppert sent Ed Barrow out to Chicago to see Landis shortly before the start of the 1922 season. Barrow later told me of his reception by the Judge.

As he was ushered into his office the Judge jumped

up and shouted, "I suppose you want to see me about that big baboon."

Barrow replied, "That's right, Judge. We and the New York fans would like to see him in our opening game."

The Judge poked a bony finger into Ed's chest and said, "Tell me something, Ed Barrow. You've been an executive in baseball and a league president. Just what would you have done if you were in my place?" Barrow squirmed unhappily, but the Judge made him answer.

"I would have done exactly as you did, Judge," Ed finally said.

The Judge then looked out of the window and said, absently, "I know what I'm in for, Ed. I walk down Michigan Boulevard and every newsboy says, 'There's that gray-haired old —— who's keeping Babe Ruth out of the game.' And that will be magnified all over the country. But if that big ape thinks I'm going to ease up on him he's got another think coming."

So Meusel and I sat it out until May 20th, and it didn't do either of us any good. We were both full of life, and if we couldn't go to the ball park there were a lot of other places we could go. It was hard staying in shape under such circumstances.

Despite our absence from the line-up, the 1922 Yankees, with a strong staff of pitchers, got off well. Cleveland, our main enemy in 1920 and 1921, dropped out of the running, but the Browns, managed by Lee Fohl, the player I knocked off the managerial bench in Cleveland, had a hot club. George Sisler, hitting .420, had his biggest season, and the Browns had three other tough hitters in Ken Williams, "Baby Doll" Jacobson and their catcher, Hank Severeid And they had one of the game's toughest pitchers, Shocker.

The Yankees met the Browns the day my suspension was lifted. I'll never forget that game. It was one in a million, for the Browns actually won it after the last man had been called out.

It was played at the Polo Grounds on a Saturday, and there was such a terrific turnout that the police shut the gates an hour before game time. A lot of fans came out to see Bob and me, but it was our second baseman, Aaron Ward, who provided the main thunder. He hit a home run with a man on base, giving us an early 2 to 0 lead on Shocker. Sam Jones was our pitcher. He gave up a run in the eighth, but retired the first two men in the ninth and we seemed to have the game won.

Then two pinch-hitters made good for the players at the bottom of the line-up. That brought up Johnnie Tobin, their fast lead-off man. Johnnie grounded down to Wallie Pipp at first, who tossed it over to Sam Jones, covering first base, and Umpire Ollie Chill thumbed Tobin out. We broke for the clubhouse while the fans in the lower stands tumbled out onto the field.

But Jones hadn't made a clean catch of the ball. Pipp's throw hit Sam's glove, took a short bounce, and by the time Sam grabbed it securely Tobin had crossed the bag.

Fohl, coaching at first, squawked to Chill and finally went to the umpire behind the plate, who admitted that Jones hadn't caught the ball when it first struck his glove and that Tobin should have been ruled safe.

From then on there was the craziest mix-up I ever saw. Some of our players already were in the showers and thought it was a gag when they were told to return to the field. "Hey, I saw Chill call that man out," I squawked, and I had plenty of company.

In the meantime the fans were milling around on the ball field, and it took the special cops about 20 minutes to clear the field.

It still makes me froth to think what happened after that. Jones had cooled off and had lost his stuff by the time he returned to the rubber. There were a couple of blooper hits and bases on balls which tied the score, and then that big Jacobson came up with the bases filled and knocked a ball into the lower right-field stands.

The Browns scored six runs after their last man had been called out, and beat us 6 to 2!

If ever there was a wild ball club it was us in the clubhouse that night. As for Jones, the loss of the game bothered him so that he went on a ten-game losing streak immediately afterward.

I wasn't much help. While my suspension limited my season to 110 games, I fell off in all departments. My batting average sank from .378 to .315, and my home runs dropped from 59 to 35. That still was a lot of homers, but it wasn't good enough to keep my home-run title that season.

Our 1922 team wasn't a harmonious club, and looking back I'm really surprised we finally won. I had my arguments with Hug and so did Hoyt, Mays and Bush. The club knew that Huston had no use for Huggins, and that didn't increase our respect for the little man.

The Yankees of that period were an odd club. I don't believe there ever was a gamer, more fighting team. We played up to the hilt in every game, but we had more than our share of night riders. We kept a couple of Jersey beer barons rich.

Barrow hired a detective to make a Western trip with us and report back to him. The gumshoe posed as a great Yankee fan who was taking the trip as a sort of vacation. He seemed to know a lot of spots we had never heard of.

Just at that time a sensitive, one-armed reporter, Bob Boyd of the *Evening World,* joined us to make his first Western trip. Bob, who was born in Australia, lost his left arm in an aviation accident while serving in the first World War and was pretty touchy about it.

Our friend, the dick, confided to us one night at a beer party that he thought we were being shadowed, and when we agreed, in our dumb way, he put the finger on the new sports writer—Boyd. That poor boy had an awful trip. We shunned him as if he were a leper.

The detective wormed his way more and more into our confidence. He apparently had plenty of money and knew drinking places to take us to in Detroit, Chicago and every other place we went. He knew about a politically protected brewery in Joliet, and took us to a party there after an exhibition game, even arranging for a photographer. He said he wanted some pictures for his den. We posed all over the place, including a shot of us leaning happily against one of the vats.

When we got back to New York, "Cap" Huston and Barrow confronted us with that picture and heavily fined everybody who was in it. It was only then that we tumbled that our nice congenial friend was the detective who was making daily reports to the club on our nightly activities. Freddie Hofmann, Meusel, Ward, Shawkey and I were fit to be tied. We never saw the dick again, and maybe it's just as well. But I can tell you that Bobby Boyd had easier traveling for the rest of the season. And, after all, we learned about a lot of new places.

About the time we came back from that trip I was still going badly, and a fan sitting in the lower stands in the Polo Grounds became particularly abusive. My ears have never been very rabbity, but I couldn't stop listening to what he called me. I stood it as long as I could. Then I opened one of the field gates and started up the stands. The guy saw me coming and beat it. He scrammed in such a hurry that he left his shoes under his seat. I chased him all the way out the speedway entrance at the Polo Grounds. It later developed that the fan was a New York Central conductor, and Bill McGeehan, the great sports columnist on the old New York *Tribune,* wrote that I chased him all the way up the tracks to Albany. Ban Johnson didn't think it was so very funny. He slapped a $100 fine on me, and I was in for another short suspension.

I had another bad experience with Ban that season and it cost me my captaincy. In a game in Cleveland, Tommy Connelly, now head of the American League umpires, called me out on what I thought was a real raw decision. Because I was in a slump, and sore, I lost my head and called Tommy a name. As a result, Johnson took away my title of captain, and, despite the efforts of the Yankees and Christy Walsh, Johnson never would restore it. For some years thereafter we had no captain on the Yankees.

We never would have won that 1922 pennant if it hadn't been for a deal Ruppert was able to work with Frazee late in July. At the time we were trailing the Browns by two games. We were weak at third base, where the great Frank Baker had finally slowed to a walk and Mike McNally was "good field—no hit!" The Colonel waved that moneybag under Frazee's nose, and the next day we had Joe Dugan, then the best third baseman in baseball, and Elmer Smith, an extra hard-hitting outfielder. That late-season deal had the St. Louis fans wild, and poor Joe was panned there for years, even though he had no more to do with the transaction than Joe Doakes.

Our winning margin in 1922 was only one game. We won the pennant on the home grounds of the Browns by taking two out of three in a rough September series. The crowd hated us so much I thought they'd come out of the stands after us when we beat their heroes.

At the time we had a little white-headed center fielder named Whitey Witt. In the first game of the series a fan in the center-field bleachers hit Whitey on the head with a bottle, and he still wears the trade mark of our 1922 visit to St. Louis on his skull today. Witt's ninth-inning single gave us the winning runs of the third and deciding game, after Fohl had rushed in Shocker in an effort to hold the St. Louis lead.

During that season a young St. Louis left-hander, "Shucks" Pruett, now a physician in St. Louis, gave me more trouble than any pitcher I ever faced. He came from the University of Missouri and never did much outside of that 1922 season. He had a dinky little curve but he could fool me with it time after time. It almost seemed that "Shucks" hypnotized me. I never looked sillier in my life than I looked when facing Pruett, swinging from the ground and hitting nothing but air. I faced him 17 times that year. He struck me out 15 times. I got one base on balls and one hit. And that hit was a home run.

Wally Pipp, our first baseman, and I had a fight on the bench that season. Some people have tried to make a lot out of this and have made it appear that Pipp gave me a good drubbing. That isn't so, as the fight was over almost before it started, with Wally landing one good punch.

The incident happened in St. Louis. I thought Wally had loafed on a ball, and when we came in to the bench I spoke to him about it. You know how you pop off now and then. We exchanged a few more words and then he pulled back his left and let me have it. I didn't know it was coming until his fist hit my chin. I tripped over the bench and went down and before I had a chance to get up and do a little swinging on my own, the whole ball club got between us. I'll say this for Pipp, however—he was mighty handy with his fists, and I'd have backed him against almost anyone in the league.

In the 1922 World Series we met the Giants for the second time. It turned out to be a deep humiliation for the Yanks, the American League and me. The only success we had in five games was a 3 to 3, 10-

inning tie, pitched by Bob Shawkey in the second game.

I came out of it, as I said, with the sorry batting average of .118, getting only one single and a double in 17 times at bat. We lost by close scores, 3 to 2, 3 to 0, 4 to 3 and 5 to 3. It is easy to see how my failure to hit let down my ball club.

People have often asked me since how a hitter of my reputation and ability could have gone through a five-game series with such a punk showing. My reply is that it was just one of those things that can happen to a regular as easily as it can happen to a sub.

Hans Wagner, Ty Cobb and Rogers Hornsby also had World Series in which they were almost as bad as I was in 1922. Ted Williams of the Red Sox was an embarrassing bust in the Cardinal-Red Sox Series of 1946.

I hit the longest ball of the depressing 1922 Series in the fourth game, but it was just a loud out. It was a ball to dead center and almost as long as those two home runs I hit into the center-field bleachers in 1921. I hit it off Hughie McQuillan. Bill Cunningham, the Giants' center fielder, caught it between the Eddie Grant monument and the center-field bleachers, if you're familiar with that park. There was just a little gap between the monument and the stand, and that darn ball, after traveling about 480 feet on the fly, had to come down at just that spot. Two runners who were on base were practically over the plate by the time Cunningham made the catch, and it was all they could do to get back to their bases without being doubled up.

We really expected to win the Series, and our rather shameful showing was a deep disappointment to us all. On paper we thought we had far the better of it in pitching. Hug had five first-string right-handers: Bush, Mays, Shawkey, Hoyt and Jones. Bush was especially good that year, winning 26 for us.

But our only decent showing was in the second game, when Shawkey and Jesse Barnes battled to that 10-inning, 3 to 3 tie. The last decision of that game was the big laugh of the Series. Ballplayers make errors, but the biggest error of that Series was made by Umpire Hildebrand when he called this game practically in the middle of the afternoon "on account of darkness." That was one of the worst boners I ever saw pulled on the ball field. There was a good half hour of daylight after that. The fans yelled bloody murder—and they should have.

Just before the game was called Hildebrand went over to Judge Landis' box and spoke to the old fellow. Because of this the fans got the idea it was Landis who ordered the game called. As the Judge walked across the field, a bunch of irate fans were at his heels calling him a crook, a robber and a lot of other unpleasant things. The Judge was so sore that he issued an order that night that all the receipts of the game should be given away to charity.

As the Series went on and we were getting it in the neck every day, a lot of bitter feeling broke out on our club. It exploded in the last game when Huggins ordered Joe Bush to walk Pep Youngs in order to get at George Kelly. Joe yelled something uncomplimentary at Huggins that the reporters and the fans in the front-row boxes could hear. After Youngs was walked, Kelly slammed Joe's next pitch for a single that broke up that ball game.

I had my own difficulties with the Giants. They gave me an awful riding all through the Series—and when I say riding, I mean with spurs. I've given out my share and usually could take it. But I thought they went a little too far, especially Jesse Barnes and Rawlings, who by this time was just a utility infielder.

Bob Meusel and I went into their clubhouse one day looking for Rawlings. I knew it was like invading a den of tigers. Earl Smith, the Giant catcher, who always had a stinging tongue, and Hughie McQuillan, the pitcher, greeted us with some barbed-wire language. They told me I wasn't so tough and that Pipp and Meusel of my own club had punched me.

"Leave Meusel and Pipp out of this," I bawled. "I'm looking for Rawlings." Jesse Barnes, the pitcher who had been in the 3 to 3 tie with Shawkey, then got into it. He moved over to me and pushed his face against mine.

"You've got a hell of a nerve coming in here squawking after what you called me when I was pitching yesterday," he said. I told him it wasn't so; I hadn't called him anything. But that made him madder.

"Don't make me out a liar, you so-and-so," he yelled.

He took off his coat and I took off mine, and we started to square off when McGraw came into the room and asked what was going on. Hughie Jennings, his coach, and a half dozen newspapermen also came between us. It ended with McGraw telling Bob and me to stay in our own clubhouse, where we belonged. But before I left I stood in the doorway and told those guys the names I didn't want them to call me. They seemed to think it was funny.

Our loss of the Series without winning a game also had repercussions in the front office. I've said before that Huston was no admirer of Huggins, and he placed much of the blame for our poor showing on the little shoulders of our pint-sized manager. In fact, down at press headquarters at the Commodore that night he announced that Miller Huggins had managed his last Yankee game.

That didn't sit so well with Ruppert, who, a few days later, at a party to the New York sports writers, said that Miller Huggins had given him two pennants, and he wasn't firing a man who had won New York's only American League championships.

The two Colonels had been seeing things from different angles for some time and a split between them was inevitable. But it was the argument over Huggins which finally brought it to a breaking point.

The winter after this unhappy World Series Huston sold his half interest in the club to Ruppert, and from that time on we had only one boss. It was a great break for Huggins. Prior to that he always knew one of the owners was gunning for him and he never was really sure of himself. Now, feeling he had one hundred percent backing, he became a different manager, and Huggins' great years as Yankee pilot really started from the time Huston sold out to Ruppert.

I had a few things to square up of my own. The newspaper guys had to write about it when I struck out in the pinch and flopped in the World Series, just as they had to report the balls I drove out of ball parks. But ballplayers have a way of accepting the good write-ups as due them, and get sore at the blasts. At the time I thought some of the boys in the press box were gunning for me. I gave some of them sharp, sarcastic answers, and had a few exchanges with several others. I guess I had what you'd call today a bad press.

It started in spring training, really. I unloaded a long string of language against the sportswriters one day in what I thought was the privacy of our locker room. But, as it turned out, John Kieran had just joined the team as a writer and had put on a Yankee uniform for a little workout. I thought he was just another fellow trying out for the club. John wasn't accustomed to such rough talk and loyally protested to the others.

At the N. Y. Elks Club that winter Christy Walsh threw a party for the writers in which we were all to let our hair down and I was to answer any questions that they wanted to put to me. I knew I had just gone through a very mediocre season and Walsh had reminded me, too, that I would be 28 on my next birthday and I would have to take myself in hand or run the danger of ending my baseball career in my early thirties.

We mapped out a course whereby I was to spend the early winter at my Massachusetts farm chopping trees, shoveling snow, and generally building myself up again. After that I was to go to Hot Springs for another training course.

At the dinner I told the sports writers what I had in mind. I admitted I often had been cross and irritable to them during the past season, and was willing to make amends. Walsh then told them they could fire questions at me and bring up some of the unpleasant incidents of the past season.

Well, they say an elephant never forgets—and those guys surely were elephants! Almost all of them had a gripe.

Kieran, Bob Kelley and one or two others took me to task. But John, then with the *Tribune,* was tops. He finished his speech by asking me why I always squawked whenever any newspaper criticism came my way and I answered, "Because when you guys write something bad about me, whether it's right or wrong, ten million people see it, but I have no way of replying except by cussing you out to my friends." John thought awhile, grinned and said, "Gee, Babe, I think you've got something there."

When it was over we all shook hands. We were pals again. They said they would be only too happy to write good things about me, and I told them that in 1923 I'd be doing my bit to give them just that kind of material.

Jimmy Walker, then a New York State Senator, and the greatest speaker I ever heard, turned to me in the course of his talk that night and gave me the greatest bawling out a man ever had. It wasn't harsh, but nothing ever impressed me as much as that lecture did.

He stressed my duty not only to my employers, but to those eager-faced kids that hung around the clubhouse entrances, and followed me in their newspapers. He stressed what I meant to those boys. The dirty-faced kids in the streets of America looked up to me as to some kind of god, Jimmy said. And then he paused a long time and broke the silence in the room itself. "Are you going to let those kids down again?" he asked.

I blubbered.

Ruth began his baseball career as a catcher (top row, left) on the St. Mary's Industrial School team, in Baltimore. (INP)

Switching to the
other side of the
plate, Ruth pitched
for the Boston
Americans. (INP)

Ruth shows pitching
form for Boston
Americans, 1916. (INP)

Over the fence! Ruth knocks his twenty-first home run of the 1920 season at Polo Grounds, New York. (INP)

Upper, Taking tender care of his trade tool, Ruth hones
bat to harden grain. (Universal)

Lower, The grip that rocked the baseball world. (U&U)

Lou Gehrig shakes Ruth's hand after homer in
third game of 1932 World Series. (INP)

Upper, Pennant winners of 1927 season. Yanks' sluggers enabled them to take league lead from opening series with Athletics to end: (left to right) Combs, Ruth, and Meusel. (U&U)

Lower, Another group of 1927 Pennant winners: (left to right) Hoyt, Ruth, Huggins, Meusel and Shawkey. (U&U)

Ruth and Gehrig on a Sheepshead Bay fishing trip,
November 10, 1927.

Pet greyhound went to Yankee park everyday
with Ruth. This picture was taken March 11, 1925. (INP)

Upper, Yanks went on barnstorming tour in 1927, with Ruth's "Bustin' Babes" playing Gehrig's "Larrupin' Lous." Christy Walsh (center) managed the coast-to-coast exhibitions. [U&U]

Lower, Ruth shakes hands with Mickey Cochrane and Frankie Frisch before start of World Series at Detroit in 1934. Dizzy Dean is at left, Schoolboy Rowe at right. (U&U)

Ruth and Jake Ruppert sign $80,000 contract in 1930. (INP)

The Ruths, Mr. and Mrs., pose before opening game between Yankees and Red Sox in 1929 when the Babe hit homer in his first time at bat. (U&U)

Upper, Fiorello H. LaGuardia, mayor of New York, admires the Yanks and Dodgers. (U&U)

Lower, Closeup.

Ruth shakes hands with Ty Cobb, then with the Athletics,
as Eddie Collins looks on; the year is 1927. (U&U)

Upper, The Babe at Los Angeles in November, 1924, on his barnstorming tour, with Eddie Hubbell, mascot of local Knights of Columbus team. (INP)

Lower, During pre-game ceremonies honoring him, Ruth poses with new generation in 1947 American Legion junior baseball intercity game between Milwaukee and Chicago, at Comiskey Park. (INP)

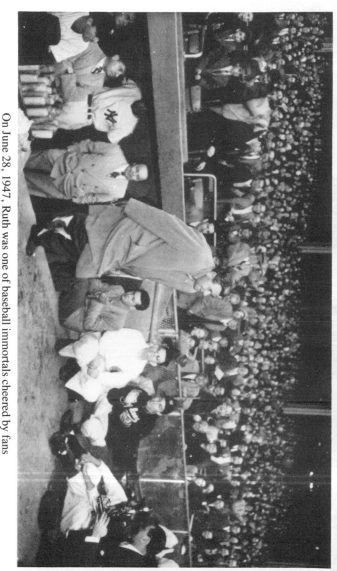

On June 28, 1947, Ruth was one of baseball immortals cheered by fans in pre-game exhibition and ceremonies. (INP)

Classic pose: the Babe as millions will always remember him best.

10

"The House That Ruth Built"

Before Huston sold out to Ruppert in the winter of 1922–23, the big new home of the Yankees was nearing completion in the Bronx. In fact, all through the season of 1922 Huston, a former Army engineer, personally saw every ton of concrete poured into the great baseball structure.

After the Yankees gave up their early home at 167th Street and Broadway in 1912, they became tenants of the Giants at the Polo Grounds, and the arrangement seemed quite satisfactory up to the time the Yankees began taking the play away from McGraw's club. So long as the Giants were top dog they had no objection to the Yankees. McGraw tolerated us, and the schedule makers naturally saw to it that we never interfered with the Giants' dates.

But as soon as the Yankees became the big draw in New York, the Giants began looking upon us as invaders.

Around 1921 Ruppert and Huston tried to buy a half interest in the Polo Grounds, and when they couldn't get it decided to build across the Harlem River, and the great Yankee Stadium, the game's largest ball park, came into being.

It was said that the big money made by the club in the years after I joined them was spent in the acquisition of the real estate and the building costs of the great structure. I don't know.

But in writing his story of the opening game of the

1923 season, Fred Lieb referred to the Yankee Stadium as "The House That Ruth Built" in the New York *Evening Telegram*. Other writers liked the phrase, and many still use it today. And I always feel proud when I see it.

Looking back at my career, and my numerous mistakes, I think I usually had good intentions. In some respects that .118 batting average in the 1922 World Series may have been a very good thing for me. I knew I let down my teammates, also the fans; and I also thought of the kids all over the country who had been watching my play in that Series. As I started training for the 1923 season I decided I wasn't going to let those youngsters down again. I was beginning to develop some kind of a sense of duty to the kids.

We trained for the second time in New Orleans. It again was a gay training season, but I was watching my step. We still were in the Prohibition era, but I recall the New Orleans chief of police throwing a crawfish party for the ball club and there was lots of beer to wash down the seafood.

We trained at the New Orleans club's ball park and usually worked out from about ten in the morning till one, after which the Pelicans took over. There was a golf course not very far from the ball park, and I still recall the look of disgust on Ed Barrow's face when he used to watch a gang of us leave the training park dressed in the golf knickers they wore at that time and carrying our golf bags. We had a number of pretty good golfers, too. Bob Shawkey was about the best at that time; but Bush, Hoyt, myself and half a dozen others were close to him.

Barrow, a baseball old-timer, couldn't understand a lot of big leaguers falling for golf. He'd stand there, look at us, and moan, "What's baseball coming to!"

Yet I think Ed was all wrong. If we hadn't gone out to the golf links we'd have gone back to our hotel, played cards in a lot of smoke-filled rooms, or we'd have gotten into trouble. We were certainly far better off out there on the golf course, toughening our legs, sharpening our eyes and breathing good clean air.

We played in Chattanooga on our way North that spring, and that suited me fine because I always seemed to get the range on Southern fences. I hit two very long home runs the day we played there.

Chattanooga, as well as some of the other Southern League parks, had cramped, little playing fields in those days. Quite a crowd turned out to see us this particular day I have in mind. They crowded along the foul lines so close to the line stripe that it was impossible to catch a foul fly, and my particular concern was that I'd pull or slice a ball into foul territory and brain somebody.

Just before that game an old fellow with whiskers down to his belly "drove" a six-year-old boy to our bench. The old guy had placed a small harness on the kid, and stood off from him, holding leather straps that led to the harness. It seemed kind of unusual, even for the Chattanooga ball park.

"Let the young 'un shake hands with you, Mr. Babe," the old guy asked me.

"Sure, Kid," I said.

I called everybody "Kid," but this time it seemed to offend somebody.

"Who you callin' Kid, me or the boy here?" the old guy demanded.

"The boy, naturally," I said.

"Just as well you did," the old fellow said. "I'm old enough to be your grandpappy."

"You're right there, Kid," was all I could think to say.

Finally we arrived in New York for the great day: the opening of the Yankee Stadium, April 18, 1923. As it was first constructed, the park seated about 65,000, but Ed Barrow managed to crowd in around 75,000 for our opening. Mayor Hylan, Judge Landis,

Big League club owners, brass hats and politicians were on hand.

We played the Red Sox, my old club. Bob Shawkey pitched for us and Howard Ehmke was the Boston pitcher. I wanted to give that crowd a run for its money, and did. In the fourth inning, with two Yanks on base, I hit a home run into the right-field bleachers, and we went on to win 4–1.

I hit a few more in there, during the next 12 years I played there. Kids will be hitting them there when I'm gone, but I'm kind of glad I hit the first one.

When those writers had me on the griddle the previous winter I promised them they'd see a new Babe Ruth in 1923. In my heart I made the same promise to the kids of the nation. And I felt I made good on my word. Though my home-run crop was 41, not nearly as many as I had when we played in the Polo Grounds in 1920 and 1921, in many respects my 1923 season was the greatest of my career. My batting average shot from .315 in 1922 to .393, the high for my 22 seasons in Big League baseball. I also had my greatest number of hits—205, the most doubles of my career— 45, and the second most triples—13.

They used to say, "As Ruth goes, so go the Yankees." This proved correct in 1923; for instead of winning the pennant by a single game, as we did in 1922, we romped home by 14 games.

I don't mean to take all of the credit. We had a great team, strengthened the winter before when Ruppert acquired about the only player of class left on Frazee's Red Sox, Herb Pennock, a truly great left-hander.

Huggins had pointed out to Ruppert that our poor showing in the 1922 World Series was due to the fact that the staff was top-heavy with right-handers. Our getting Pennock gave Miller one of the great pitching staffs of all time.

When the Yanks bought Pennock from Boston they

tossed in several of our ballplayers with the purchase money, one of them my good friend Lefty O'Doul, now manager of the San Francisco Seals. I was very fond of Lefty, and in my early days with the Yankees he and Freddie Hofmann, the second-string catcher, were among my closest pals.

O'Doul was a good-natured Irishman from San Francisco and full of life. It was always fun to be with him, and still is. He could hit and run, and eventually became a National League batting champion; but at that early stage of his career Huggins was undecided as to whether to develop him into a left-handed pitcher or an outfielder.

After two setbacks, we finally smacked down the Giants in the 1923 World Series, and it was a happy occasion for Ruppert, Huggins and the entire team. We not only opened our new park with our third American League pennant, but with our first World Series championship.

I had a good series. I hit .368 and drove out three home runs. Oddly enough, we lost two of the three games played at the Stadium, but won all three at the Polo Grounds.

Casey Stengel, one of the daffiest guys I ever met, was responsible for both of the Giant victories. He hit a ninth-inning home run to give McGraw a 5 to 4 victory in the first game, and his home run into the right-field bleachers decided a 1 to 0 pitching duel between Sam Jones and Artie Nehf in the third game.

We had a lot of fun with Casey all through the Series. There never was anything abusive about him. We rode him just to hear his clownish comebacks. I know I kidded him plenty. And when he won the 1 to 0 game he ran around the bases with his thumb to his nose and his hand pointed toward the Yankee bench. I think it was meant for me in particular as he tried to show me he, too, knew how to hit home runs.

Ruppert didn't like it and later said it was undignified. But we didn't mind Casey having his fun.

The first three games we won were won decisively: 8 to 4, 8 to 1 and 4 to 1. We were leading in the Series, three games to two, when McGraw sent in Nehf in the hope of tying it up for him. It looked as if Artie was going to get away with it, for he was leading 4 to 1 in the eighth and we had made only two hits, including my homer in the first inning. But suddenly, in the eighth inning, we got into the ball game, and before one of our happiest innings and McGraw's saddest was over we had scored five runs, which gave us the ball game and the Series.

Nehf blew his top when our first two hitters, Schang and Scott, singled. He suddenly lost his control and threw eight straight balls to two pinch hitters, Joe Bush and Fred Hofmann. That forced in a run. McGraw called in Rosy Ryan, who was a pretty sweet relief pitcher, but he also started wild, walking Dugan, which forced in another run and left us only one behind.

I was the next man up. I would have given my season's salary to have pumped one of Rosy's curves into the stands. But he struck me out. They say I was so anxious to hit at that last strike that I struck at a ball that hit the dirt in front of the plate. That's an exaggeration, though if I hadn't swung at it, it surely would have been a ball.

I fell down in the pinch, but my pal, Bob Meusel didn't. He hit a high bouncer in front of the plate. It hopped over Ryan's head and bounced out into center field. Lee King got hold of it and threw wildly to third, and by the time the boys stopped running we'd scored three more big runs and eventually won the ball game 6 to 4.

It was the first time the Yankees ever had a chance to celebrate a World Series victory, and Ruppert surely did it up brown. He threw a tremendous party at the Commodore, and a few of the boys got kind of dizzy before a very happy night was over.

For years some of the mimics of the club would recite Ruppert's victory speech. There was a reporter, Harry Newman, then of the *Daily News,* who gave it perfectly. Though born in New York, Colonel Ruppert spoke with a pronounced German accent, and he always pronounced "Ruth" as though it were spelled "Root." In his speech Jake said, "This is a wonderful occasion. I now have baseball's greatest park, baseball's greatest player, and baseball's greatest team. We had a great Series and Babe 'Root,' Wardie, Meusel, Bush and Shawkey all had great Series. But let's give credit where credit is due and give most credit to little Hug."

At the end of the 1923 season, one of the great honors of my career came to me. I won the American League's Most Valuable Player award. It was not the winning of the award which pleased me so much, but how I won it. I got 64 votes out of a possible 64. First place then received eight votes, and each of the committeemen put me first on their ballot. Ty Cobb, in 1911, and I in 1923, were the only players ever to win these awards with a perfect score. It made me feel I had made up for 1922.

I can't leave the 1923 season without telling about a husky, big-framed Dutchman who came to the Yankee Stadium in June of that year. He had been a football and baseball player at Columbia, and his name was Lou Gehrig. He was then a green kid, bashful and backward, but he developed into one of baseball's greatest all-time stars, and I believe I am not stretching it when I say we later constituted the greatest one two punch in baseball history.

Lou stayed with us only a few weeks in 1923. I watched him at batting practice, and after seeing him clout a couple into the bleachers, I said to someone standing near, "That kid sure can bust 'em." One of the reporters apparently overheard it and started calling him "Buster" Gehrig. It didn't stick as much as his later nicknames of "The Iron Horse" and "Larrupin' Lou." But for years many did call him "Buster" Gehrig.

Barrow farmed him to Hartford for July and August, but he was back with us in September of 1923 and hit over .400 for about a dozen games as a first baseman.

Lou almost made his first World Series that same fall. Pipp cracked a rib late that season and the Yankees asked Landis' permission to play young Gehrig. The Judge put it up to McGraw, who growled, "No." So our trainer taped up Pipp and he played a fine Series.

No American League club had ever won four straight pennants. Jennings' Tigers had won three in a row in 1907, 1908 and 1909, but were tripped when they went after their fourth in 1910. After our easy victory and World's Championship in 1923, we fondly expected in 1924 to become the first American League four-in-a-row club. However, we just couldn't quite make it. For most of the season we figured we had Ty Cobb's Tigers to beat, but a rejuvenated Washington club, led by the then boy manager, Bucky Harris, never was far behind. The Senators closed strongly, and in a hot September finish nosed us out by 2½ games.

Washington's victory was one of the greatest surprises of baseball up until that time. Back in the spring we never gave them a thought. We had finished about 25 games ahead of them in 1923, when Donie Bush ran the club for Clark Griffith.

But clubs change quickly from one season to another, and Washington got hot quicker than almost any club I ever saw. Bucky's team that year had some familiar faces, and one of them was Roger Peckinpaugh, who played like crazy against us. He was still sore about the deal which traded him away from us after the 1921 World Series, and no man on Harris' club did more to beat us in 1924.

Bucky Harris, the "Boy Wonder" of 1924, who won a pennant in his first year in charge of the Senators, is, of course, the same guy who, in 1947, won a championship in his first year in command of the Yankees and went on to beat the Dodgers in just about the daffiest Series I ever saw.

Even if it was a disappointment for me not to play on another pennant winner, I look back on that 1924 season with considerable pleasure. I led the American League that year with a batting average of .378, and I got a big kick out of seeing my name at the head of the parade, in front of the likes of Ty Cobb, Harry Heilmann, George Sisler, Eddie Collins and the other fine hitters of that period. I also did pretty good in the home-run department, poking out 46, my third best season up to that time.

It was around this time that one of those professors up in Columbia gave me a series of tests after which one of the New York newspapers pronounced me one man out of a million. It seemed I scored over 90 percent in all-round coordination, which is far above the average. He showed that my eyesight was far better than normal; only one person in six had as good vision as I had then. The same was true of my hearing. I scored even higher in nervous stability. For this I was one man in five hundred. This was termed "speed of recovery." The spade-beard put me through all sorts of capers in physical and mental reactions, and I scored outstandingly in all departments. He felt it was the combination of my high marks in all his tests which made me what he called "unusual."

I know my limitations as well as the things I was good at. In schooling I wasn't the smartest guy who ever played baseball. But baseball men said I had keen intuition, and reporters who followed the Yankees for years say they never recall seeing me make a wrong play. I just used to sense those things. I'd often take a terrific swing at a ball and miss it a mile, but the very next time the pitcher would try that same pitch there was a pretty good chance that I would connect.

As I succeeded in baseball and the big money began coming in from my outside interests, I never got reckless enough to forget St. Mary's Brother Matthias and the kids I left behind me in Baltimore. I kept going back. Most of the boys I knew had left, the great majority of them to become useful citizens in the outside world. But other kids slept in our old beds, worked at our old benches, played in the same yard, and my heart was with them. I sent money down to the school, and when some of their school buildings burned I took the St. Mary's boys band on a Western trip with the Yankees. They'd play concerts—and those kids really could play—and then take up a collection through the stands. The fans were most liberal, and those good-will offerings were a big factor in erecting the new and better buildings now at St. Mary's.

At a time during '24 when Detroit looked like the club for us to beat we staged the most riotous scene in which I ever participated. It was at Navin Field in Detroit. There had been considerable ill-feeling between the clubs all through the game, and the thing exploded in the ninth. We were leading 10 to 6. We had knocked out Lil Stoner, and Cobb was pitching Leonard Cole, known to ballplayers as King Cole.

Cobb was managing from center field, and as Bob Meusel went to bat I believed I caught Ty's sign for Cole to dust off Meusel with an inside pitch. I tipped Bob off to look out for a ball that would be thrown at him, and, sure enough, Bob was hit in the small of the back. Bob was one of those silent guys who never said much but when he was mad he just boiled over.

He threw his bat at Cole's head and charged out at him on the mound.

I could see Cobb tearing in from the outfield and I rushed at him like a football player trying to knock an opposing man out of the play. Within the next few minutes that ball field was a shambles, with everybody throwing punches. Meusel challenged the entire club, and the Tiger third baseman, Freddie Haney, later manager of the Browns, was swinging at anyone within reach. Cobb and I were poking at each other, a picture I wish I had for this book.

The crowd decided this wasn't a private fight between the Yankees and the Tigers. About a thousand swarmed out of the stands and declared themselves in.

You never saw such a rough-house. The fans were swinging at us, at the cops and at one another. They even ripped seats out of the grandstand and threw them into the general fight. The situation was so bad that there seemed no chance of getting the crowd off the field; so Billy Evans forfeited the game to us by a score of 9 to 0.

The league president, Ban Johnson, went wild when he got the reports. Bob Meusel was socked with a $100 fine and suspended for ten days. King Cole and I got off with $50 fines. The amusing part of it was that the next day a capacity crowd of 40,000 jammed into the stands, hoping for a repetition of the battle royal, but all was peace and quiet.

Huggins brought up Earle Combs, a great outfielder, in this 1924 season. Hug put him in center field in place of Whitey Witt, and for about a month Earle tore up the league, hit .400 and stole a flock of bases. Then he broke a leg which was the chief reason why Washington won its first pennant.

Combs was more than a grand ballplayer. He was always a first-class gentleman. No one ever accused him of being out on a drinking party and you'd laugh at the words he used for cussing. Often he'd sit in his room and read the Bible, for he came from a strict mountaineer family. But Earle was all man, and a great competitor.

I've said before that Duffy Lewis, Tris Speaker and Harry Hooper, my old Red Sox associates, made a pretty sweet outfield, and many termed them the greatest of them all. But later on, when Earle Combs played between Bob Meusel and myself, I think our outfield rated even a little higher. We were so much more dangerous on the attack.

Except that Combs didn't have Speaker's arm, he could do everything as well as "Spoke." A left-handed hitter like myself, he had the faculty of driving the balls to center field, left center, and right field, and nobody ever drove a ball back any harder at a pitcher. We had to put up a low net in front of our batting-practice pitchers so he wouldn't cut them down.

Earle was the perfect lead-off man. He'd get on somehow, and with his speed he could score on almost any kind of hit by the big boys who followed him in our line-up.

11

How to Hit the Bottom

As a young man I found it hard to stand prosperity. I changed from batting champion in 1924 to the big bust of 1925. My batting average caved in to .290 and in 98 games I had the rather sad runs-driven-in total of 66. I hit only 25 homers and Bob Meusel dethroned me as home-run king.

This is no alibi, but some outside forces helped bring on my collapse that year. I should have had strength enough to overcome some of the temptations, but as it turned out I didn't.

The 1920's seemed to be full of fair-weather friends and I wound up with most of them. The papers and the radio and the record books had built me into a big figure. A lot of free-spending people liked to be around me, and at the time it seemed like fun to be around them. I was young and healthy and saw no reason why I could not play both day and night. I got so many invitations to go here or there that I used to forget the names of the people who invited me. But I'd go.

The Yankees trained for the first time in St. Petersburg, Fla., in 1925. There is supposed to be an annual roundup of old geezers and grandmothers at St. Pete every winter. The place does attract a lot of oldsters, but a strong guy of 28—with his name in the headlines—doesn't have much trouble kicking up some dust in any town.

For about the next twelve years I made it my winter

headquarters and rarely found time hanging heavily on my hands. I golfed, fished and took part in the other joys of that hospitable town.

We were a new experience to St. Petersburg when we first arrived there in 1925. I got in a few days before the ball club arrived. So did a couple of newspaper guys: my little shadow, Marshall Hunt, and Dan Parker, then a long, skinny guy of about 150 pounds.

Having finished a strong second in 1924 and having acquired Urban Shocker, the crack Brown pitcher, we again looked like the favorites for the pennant in 1925.

But if Washington dazzled the nation in 1924 by winning its first pennant, we certainly shocked the country in 1925 when we nose-dived to seventh place, the only Yankee club to finish in the second division in the last thirty years. I had a terrible season and the ball club rolled down the hill with me. But the crack-up was hardly noticeable at first.

Maybe a good ball club was breaking up, but no one thought so when we broke training camp and started on our usual long barnstorming trip back to the Stadium.

Several days after leaving St. Pete I wasn't feeling any too well, but thought little of it. It seemed like just another one of those troubles that can be cured with a bromide. So I didn't watch my diet, and in addition to regular meals I stoked in a lot of hot dogs, cokes, and other refreshments.

The night before we came into Chattanooga I was playing hearts with Scottie, Steve O'Neill, who had joined us that year as catcher, and a few of the other boys. I felt awful but went on with the game. When we arrived at the hotel in Chattanooga on a Sunday morning I told Huggins I felt sick and asked him to get me a doctor. The house physician came up and said I had a temperature of 102 and that I'd better stay in bed that day.

Before Huggins left for the park he came into my

room and ordered me to stay in bed until we left town. That suited me, and I lay back on the pillow and tried to go to sleep. But it was no use.

Maybe it will sound a bit conceited, but I always felt I had an obligation to my public. I knew from the local papers, the phone calls, mail and the yells of the people at the train stations and hotels that fans in the South were buying tickets to our games in the hope of seeing me hit a long one. I fussed and fretted in bed, and about a half hour before the game I got up and put on my monkey suit, stumbled into a taxicab and told the driver to get me out to the ball park by two-thirty if he had to go through every red light in town.

Once again the Chattanooga ball park was jammed, right to the sidelines. I actually had to fight my way through hundreds of people who were crowding the aisles and were massed behind our bench. Not only did I have to shove my way through, but half of them wanted to shake hands or slap me on the back. Finally, when I did shoulder my way to our bench, Huggins greeted me with a glare.

"What the hell are you doing here? Didn't I tell you to stay in bed today?"

"Sure you did, Hug," I said, "but I just couldn't let all these people down." Hug thought that over for a while.

"All right; play five innings," he said. I played five innings, drove two long home runs out of the park, and then arranged with Mark Roth, our road secretary, for a taxicab to take me back to the hotel.

I left Chattanooga with the ball club that night and went to bed early, though I got little sleep. Our next game was scheduled in Asheville, N. C., and we were due to get in shortly before noon. To pass away the time I again got into a hearts game, though I felt hot all over and knew I was burning up with fever. Then it happened.

In the Asheville station I was walking with Steve O'Neill on our way to a taxicab when suddenly I pitched forward. I would have fallen to the floor if Steve hadn't reached out and grabbed me. With some other players he helped me into a cab and I was taken to our hotel and then, when it was realized I was very sick, to a hospital. It was what the reporters called "the stomach ache that was heard around the world." But I was sicker than that.

It was evident that it would be some weeks before I again would play any baseball, and I was rushed back to New York and placed in St. Vincent's Hospital. About half the reporters who were assigned to the Yankees stayed over in Asheville with me and went back to New York on the same train, issuing bedside bulletins at every telegraph stop.

I was a mighty sick man. But I doubt if I was as seriously ill as some of the writers made me out to be. Some newspapers and radio stations gave out early reports that I was dying. There even was one report circulated in Europe that I had died.

While I was convalescing in St. Vincent's Hospital someone brought me a two-column obituary of me, printed in a London newspaper. My illness was no funny matter, but I sure had to laugh at that English sports reporter's views of me and my part in American baseball. Some of our guys used their imaginations, but this English fellow pulled out all the stops.

It was May before I was able to rejoin the club, pale, weak and unsteady on my legs. After playing one game I returned to the hospital, but was back with the club a day or so later. Only occasionally could I get any of my old punch into a swing.

In the meantime a lot of bad things were happening to our supposeuly solid ball club. Everett Scott, who was a teammate of mine on my early Red Sox champions, had a remarkable consecutive game streak which had started away back in June, 1916. I don't know how long Scottie could have gone on with his streak, but Hug saw that he had slowed up, was no longer getting the balls he formerly did, and benched him on May 6, 1925. Everett had played 1307 consecutive games.

Hug put a little runt of an infielder, Peewee Wanninger, in at short in Scottie's place. And here came about one of the oddest coincidences in baseball. Scottie's streak was far longer than any in the record books up to that time. None of us ever expected to see that record broken. Yet within less than a month Lou Gehrig, our youmg first baseman, started on another streak which was to leave Scottie's mark far behind.

On June 1st Hug sent Lou in to pinch-hit for little Wanninger, the guy who took over from Scottie. Pipp, our regular first baseman, showed up with a headache the next day, and Huggins walked over to young Gehrig.

"You take over at first base today, Lou," Hug said, and none of us realized we were listening to history in the making.

Wally never got back. Lou ran off a streak of 2130 games which ended so sadly in 1939, when the great Iron Horse was mowed down by the disease that eventually killed him.

After my early season's illness and subsequent slump this was one season when I should have watched my step. I didn't. The reader can imagine the mental attitude which existed on our club. Here was a team which had run first for three straight years, and then was just nosed out of a fourth straight pennant, and was now wallowing in the depths of the second division. We rarely got above seventh. We griped and snapped at one another, but mostly at our little manager.

A manager with a team such as ours doesn't look too good with his team running next to last, and some of the hotheads on the club didn't make it any easier for him. He pitched hard into Bob Meusel and me while we were on a westbound train one day. We were in the rear end of the observation car and I picked him up like a doll and held him over the rail. It was a nutty thing to do, but Hug forgave me that one. I don't know why.

Going into August I was hitting a sorry .246. We were playing in St. Louis, where I always had a lot of high-living friends. I forgot to come home to my room in the Chase Hotel for a couple of nights, and I didn't get away with it.

After my second night out, I showed up at the ball park late that day—after the club had taken batting practice. I started to rip off my clothes and reach for my uniform when Huggins came in. His face was flushed with anger.

"I'm sorry I'm late, Hug," I said. "Had some personal business to attend to."

You could have heard his snort as far as the bleachers.

"You've had too much personal business lately, Babe," he snapped. "And what's more, don't bother dressing today."

I couldn't believe it.

"Why not?" I asked him.

"You know damn well why not," Hug shouted. "What's more, I'm fed up with your excuses. This time you've gone too far. You're suspended indefinitely, and I've got some more news for you—you're fined $5000."

Well, I hit the roof.

"Why, you little runt," I said, coming over to him with my toughest look, "if you were fifty pounds heavier I'd knock your brains out."

He looked up at me, just as tough, and yelled "And it's just as well for you the I'm *not* fifty pounds heavier."

"You can't do this to me," I bawled. "I'll go to New York and see Ruppert and—"

"That's what I want you to do," Huggins broke in. "And I'd just like to be there when you bust into Ruppert's office, carrying that .246 batting average and telling him I'm picking on you." He turned on his heel and left me there, steaming and tongue-tied.

Maybe I did overrate my place in the Yankee organization. I had read so many articles eulogizing me, received daily hundreds of letters from persons all over the world, was still greeted by thousands of kids wherever I went, and I suppose I got the idea that I could do no wrong.

I got indignant for the benefit of every reporter who interviewed me at station stops on the train ride to New York. At first I was pretty critical of Hug and accused him of some dumb plays. I said something foolish to the effect that I never would play for the Yankees again so long as Huggins was in command, and that Hug was trying to alibi for his seventh-place showing. I sputtered that Ruppert would have to decide between me and Huggins. But as the train neared New York I toned down.

I later got the low-down on this fine and suspension. Ruppert wasn't even consulted at the start. The club had me shadowed for two nights before the storm broke. Barrow was in Saratoga at the time, a guest of Harry Stevens, the concessionaire whose fine sons, Frank, Joe, Harold and Bill, and their sons, I still number among my best friends.

Barrow got a call from Huggins in St. Louis and Huggins immediately popped, "I want to fine that big ape."

Barrow, surprised that Hug was calling him on such a matter, replied "Well, it's all right with me."

But Huggins continued, "I want to fine him $5,000. He hasn't been in the hotel the last two nights. And this fine's got to stick. I want you to see that Ruppert stands behind me on this."

"It isn't necessary to go to Ruppert," Ed answered. "If I am in back of you that is all that is necessary. I'll see this thing through with you."

Well, by the time I reached Ruppert's brewery at the end of my trip I knew I wasn't the Prodigal Son. The only welcomers were a bunch of reporters and photographers who were in Jake's outer office, waiting for the killing.

When I was ushered into Jake's office, Barrow was in there with him. Between them they did a great job of taking the wind out of my sails. Ruppert was the man who was paying me baseball's top salary and I couldn't talk to him as I did to Huggins. They didn't give me much chance to talk about Huggins, but submitted some reports from their operatives in the West.

I quickly was given to understand that Huggins was boss on the ball club and that I was just another player. What's more, I was told my suspension would last until such time as Huggins lifted it.

When Barrow opened the door to let in the reporters I no longer was cocky. Ruppert said, "Gentlemen, I think maybe Babe 'Root' has changed his mind and will continue playing for Mr. Huggins. That's right, isn't it 'Root'?"

"Yes," I muttered.

Ruppert continued, "Babe 'Root' is sorry for this whole thing. We all regret this unfortunate situation. But I believe 'Root' has had a lesson that will sink in."

Someone then asked when my suspension would be lifted. "That's entirely up to Mr. Huggins," replied Jake. "Whenever he wants to put 'Root' back in the line-up it's all right with me. But I am giving him no suggestions."

Another reporter broke in and asked, "What about the fine, Colonel?" Ruppert closed his jaw and said,

"Gentlemen, that fine sticks—and I mean it." He wasn't kidding. That fine did stick, at least for the next four years, and it wasn't rescinded until after Huggins' death in the last week of the 1929 season.

I am not proud of this chapter of my baseball life. It is one of those things a man would like to change if he could alter the past. But men and boys learn from experience, and I believe I learned something from this one. I knew that although Huggins was a little man in stature, he was the boss, and I had acted like a spoiled child.

When the team returned to New York I apologized to Huggins and promised him that I would do better, and he soon returned me to the line-up.

In the remaining games that I played in late August and September I did my best playing of the year, even boosting my batting average up to .290. But what a year!

12

My Seventh Pennant Winner

All during my career I had the ability to bounce back quickly. The Yankees had that same resilience. From a seventh-place club in 1925 we dumbfounded the critics by winning the pennant in 1926. It was my seventh championship club.

I still take a lot of credit for my foresight that season. In the spring I had the nerve to pick the Yankees as pennant winners. The only other guy who had the crust to go out on this limb was Fred Lieb, who also picked us in his column in the *Telegram*. Everybody said we were nuts.

I didn't pick the 1926 Yankees on sentiment. There were some excellent reasons why we were a vastly improved ball club. A lot of us were out to make comebacks, including myself.

In the early winter of 1925–26 Christy Walsh took me to the New York gymnasium of Artie McGovern. Artie was a pretty good lightweight in his day, never a champion, but a fellow handy with his dukes. He was a distant relative of the great fighter, Terry McGovern. McGovern ran a high-class gym which a lot of business executives frequented. He really knew how to condition men.

McGovern prescribed a hard series of exercises. He started fairly easy but put on the pressure as days wore on. McGovern wasn't a dumbbell man, but he knew how to stir circulation in vital organs, melt off fat, and get a fellow in condition. He had me ride bicycles, do leg exercises, and he'd throw a medicine ball at my belly until it was red and sore. But when I left there in February he had me as hard as nails and really in wonderful condition. For the next eight years winter training with Artie was a regular routine with me.

It was by going to McGovern's gym that I also became acquainted with Dr. H. Austin Cossitt. He was a specialist on glands and the digestive tract. McGovern sent me to him and he quickly learned I had collected a fine series of germ life in my intestines. I think a lot of it contributed to my poor play and rotten disposition the year before.

Dr. Cossitt and his staff got rid of the germs. It was a job. In the course of moving around the country eating tons of this and that, I had committed a kind of internal hari-kiri.

Another thing that contributed to our 1926 comeback was a successful operation on the knee of Joe Dugan, our great third baseman. The Yankees had not yet developed their farming system, but the scouts brought in two crack infielders, shortstop Mark Koenig from St. Paul and Tony Lazzeri, a tough San Francisco Italian who had hit a lot of home runs in Salt Lake City in the 1925 season. Lazzeri never had been east of the Rocky Mountains until he arrived at our 1926 St. Petersburg training camp.

Tony was a blacksmith's son, and though he weighed only 165 pounds he could hit a ball about as far as any man in the game. He had great wrists. He was a tough fellow, was afraid of nothing and nobody, and he put the fear of Lazzeri into many players 25 to 35 pounds heavier.

Lou Gehrig also came fast that season. After he took Pipp's place the previous June he finished with a .295 batting average and 21 home runs. But that was only a sample of what Lou was to produce in subsequent years. Like me, the big Dutchman batted left-handed, and to the end of his career pitchers still were trying to find his weakness. I knew Lou was a great admirer of mine; though at first he was very timid about mixing with me. I came to love that big Dutchman like a brother, told him everything I knew about hitting, and between us we gave a lot of pitchers a lot of bad afternoons.

We trained at St. Petersburg for the second time that spring. The Boston Braves also were training there, and in our early spring games they gave us an awful tossing around. In one game they beat us by something like 21 to 3. I know our playing left a terrible smell in the ball park that afternoon. We were awful.

Westbrook Pegler looked us over that afternoon and wrote a column in which he gave us a beautiful blistering. He said we were the worst club he had seen in Florida; that nobody liked Huggins, and that nobody liked each other. And he wasn't at all sure about my reformation. He pointed out that we had finished seventh in 1925 and predicted that we'd finish last in 1926.

When that column hit St. Pete we were all fighting mad. But Peg said later that he "abused us into winning" and I guess he had something there. After his piece appeared there was no stopping us.

We took on Uncle Robbie's Brooklyns and smacked them all over the South. We still were knocking them down daily when we wound up the series in Brooklyn after having won twelve straight games.

I remember especially one of our exhibitions against the Dodgers in Knoxville. Vance was pitching. I always liked big Dazz. He was a good guy, knew a lot of funny stories, and at that time had the fastest ball in the National League. But his speed didn't bother me—I had seen Walter Johnson—and in this Knoxville game I drove a ball far over right field which went through a tree some distance in back of the ball park. The tree was filled with colored kids who were watching the game from the branches, and as my home run went through that tree those boys dropped out of it like ripe apples.

The momentum of our training-game victories still carried us forward after the season got under way, and a spring winning streak of 16 straight gave us a big early season lead.

By midseason we were far in front, and galloped into September leading by 10 games. It looked like a cinch for us. But we stumbled through September while the Cleveland club came like a house on fire.

The last town we visited in the West was Cleveland, and they almost tore down the fences as we played the Indians a six-game series. We were four games ahead when we went to Cleveland and the Indians had the town crazy when they won a double-header. But we again rebounded, and finally won the series, 4 to 2. We each had a few games left after that, and eventually we won our pennant by a three-game margin.

Fortunately, Ed Barrow picked up pitcher Dutch Ruether from Washington and catcher Hank Severeid from the Browns late in the season, and they came to our rescue when it looked as if we were about to blow our lead in the last two weeks of the season.

From my weak .290 hitting season of 1925 I leaped back in the batting averages to .372 and drove in 155 runs, the fourth highest of my career. I also scored 139 runs and hit 30 doubles, 5 triples, and 47 homers.

Several times that season Huggins complimented me on my good behavior and the way I had snapped back.

"Babe," he told me once, "I admire a man who can win over a lot of tough opponents; but I admire even more a man who can win over himself." It made me feel real good.

"That's fine, Hug. Do I get the fine back?" I asked.

"No," Hug said. He wasn't a man who wasted words.

I really was beginning to become very fond of little Hug and had more respect for him than ever before. If he complimented me on my comeback, I always admired him for the way he was able to pick up that seventh-place 1925 club and in one year whip it into another pennant winner.

I said before that Bill Carrigan was for me the perfect manager; but Huggins did a grand job that year.

We met the St. Louis Cardinals for the first time in the World Series that year. The Cardinals had been one of the door-mat teams of the National League, but the Branch Rickey system was beginning to make itself felt, and with Rogers Hornsby playing and managing the Cards won their first pennant in a close race with Cincinnati and Pittsburgh. Their pennant was made possible by the midseason acquisition of the great Grover Cleveland Alexander from the Chicago Cubs. Aleck, or "Ol' Pete," as they called him, couldn't get along in Chicago with Joe McCarthy, later my manager in New York, and St. Louis gained this valuable pitcher for almost nothing.

Aleck was a prize headache for us in the big Series. Without him we would have won rather easily. He was the big rock in our path and, eventually, the deciding factor in the St. Louis Series victory.

There was another guy on the St. Louis team who was poison for us, and that was the little Cardinal shortstop, Tommy Thevenow. In the regular season's averages he ranked last of the regular players on both clubs; but in the World Series he came out top man, with a batting average of .417. He even clipped a home run at the Stadium, and that was a funny one.

There used to be a gap in right field between the stands and the bleachers that the baseball writers referred to as "Bloody Angle." Tommy hit a ball in there; and while most of the 65,000 fans in the stands could see the ball, I couldn't find it. I kept groping around for the ball which was never more than a foot away from me, while little Tommy ran around the bases.

I must have made quite a sight bawling "Where's that blankety-blank ball?" at the top of my lungs, and not a son-of-a-gun out there would tell me!

From a personal standpoint it was a good Series. Hornsby had his pitchers walk me a great deal. But even so I managed to get six hits, four of them homers, in 20 times at bat, and hit an even .300.

My good friend, Herb Pennock, was swell in that Series, and he opened up by winning a 2 to 1 game at the Stadium in which he gave up only three hits. He beat Bill Sherdel, another left-hander, who pitched well against us in two Series, but never could win a game.

Alexander clamped down on us in the second game, which the Cardinals won over Shocker, 6 to 2. After the second inning we never got a man on base. After that the schedule called for us to play the next three games in Sportsman's Park, St. Louis. We got off to a poor start there when old Jesse Haines shut us out with five hits by a score of 4 to 0, beating Dutch Ruether.

Fred Lieb, who was also doing some work for the Christy Walsh syndicate, had breakfast with me on the morning of the fourth game. We were talking about Haines' game, and Fred commented that Haines had pitched a great game.

"I don't think he pitched a smart game at all," I told him. "He was pitching right into my groove all day. He was pitching right where I liked them, but I couldn't get anything safe. I'll tell you one thing though, if they pitch that way to me again today I'll knock two out of the park."

Well, I did even a little better. I knocked three out of Sportsman's Park that afternoon. It was one of the real high spots of my career. The first two were made off Flint Rhem, a big, rawboned South Carolinian who could fog them through and who had won 20 games for Hornsby that year. But I always liked speed. I drove the first one over the right-field pavilion and it was fair by only a few feet.

My second one went over the pavilion roof well in right center. By the time I came up again, Herman Bell was pitching, and this time I really did get hold of it. They still call it the longest ball ever hit in St. Louis. It hit well up in the center-field bleachers, climbed up the seats, hopped over the wall, and finally was brought to a stop by the wall of the Y.M.C.A. across the street.

With the aid of my three homers Hoyt won this game in a breeze, 10 to 5, and we evened up the Series.

Before we left St. Louis Herb Pennock again gave us a 3 games to 2 lead by winning the fifth game in 10 innings from Sherdel by a score of 3 to 2.

We were a happy gang, going back to New York and needing only one more game to clinch the Series. We couldn't conceive of losing two games on our home grounds. But we didn't take into consideration how tough Alexander was going to be.

When we resumed at Yankee Stadium, it was a cold, raw Saturday. Huggins started Shawkey against Alexander, but Bob was quickly knocked out and Urban Shocker, who followed, was little better. "Ol' Pete" just walked in by a score of 10 to 2, and the Cardinals had the Series tied up at 3 and 3.

That put everything up to the final game on Sunday. It rained during the morning and cold blasts swept across the town. About 11 A.M. somebody sent out word that Judge Landis had called the game, but then shortly after noon we got word that Landis had ordered us to play if it was at all possible. And because of this uncertainty as to whether there would be a game many New Yorkers missed seeing one of the historic contests of baseball history. Only about 40,000 people showed up.

Jesse Haines, the old guy who shut us out in St. Louis, was their starting pitcher against Waite Hoyt, and I got the Yankees off to an early 1 to 0 lead with my fourth homer of the Series. However, in the third inning our club, which usually played a tight game in the field, went to pieces. Hoyt should have retired the side without a run; but there was a combination of boots and other fielding lapses. Meusel muffed a fly, another one fell between Bob and Koenig, and Koenig messed up a ground ball.

We picked up a second run on a double by Severeid, but our big chance to win the game and the Series came in the seventh, with the score 3–2 against us.

It was one of baseball's unforgettable innings. Combs led off for us with a single, and Koenig pushed him to second with a sacrifice. Then they gave me another one of those intentional passes that used to tear my guts out when I was itching to get hold of another home-run pitch. Bob Meusel, who still followed me in the batting order, forced me at second, Combs taking third. Then Hornsby ordered an intentional pass for big Gehrig, filling the bases with two outs.

Haines was complaining of a blister on a finger and kept looking at his hand and shaking it. Hornsby finally came to the pitcher's box, talked to him a bit, and then beckoned out to the bull pen in left field for a relief pitcher.

We had seen old Aleck trudge out there a few innings before, but two or three younger and fresher Cardinal throwers were warmed up and ready to step in—and we could hardy believe it when the old fellow himself came through the bull-pen gate and started walking slowly toward the infield.

Aleck had not only pitched a full nine-inning game

the day before but he was 40 years old at that time and had celebrated his Saturday victory as only he could celebrate. He could go longer and louder than even I could.

Hornsby met him in short left field and stopped him. For a long time Hornsby looked Aleck sharply in the eyes, and whatever he saw satisfied him. For he let him go the rest of the way to the box.

Our hitter was Tony Lazzeri. Tony's batting average in his first year wasn't so high, but he ranked next to me in runs batted in. All during his career he was toughest in a pinch, and there never had been a pinch like this one.

Aleck threw a few to get the range and then indicated that he was ready. Tony took a toe hold on the plate. Aleck delivered a fast ball and the umpire called it ball one. It was close.

The decision hurt "Ol' Pete" and we could see it on his wrinkled face. He walked up to the plate and said very quietly to the umpire, "I've been pitching 20 years in baseball. You might have given me that one."

The ump shook his head and old Aleck walked back to the mound. His next pitch was called a strike. With the count 1 and 1, Tony then hit a blazing line drive into the left-field stands, but it just curved foul.

If the ball had been fair, it would have meant four runs, and Tony would have been the hero of the year. But it missed. That is baseball. The count on Tony was two strikes and one ball.

Alexander then wound up and pitched again. Lazzeri swung with everything he had, but missed it for a clean strike-out.

We didn't get a hit off Alexander in the eighth and ninth innings. I was the last man to get on base, walking with two out in the ninth, my twelfth walk of the Series. I guess I again did something rash. I tried to steal second, but was thrown out by Bob O'Farrell, and that ended us.

Ed Barrow once said that this was the only dumb play he ever saw me make. He felt that with such hitters as Bob Meusel and Lou Gehrig coming up, anything could have happened. But my thought in going down was to pull the unexpected on O'Farrell, and, if I succeeded, to put the "tying run" in scoring position.

If it was an occasion for great rejoicing in Hornsby's clubhouse, we certainly were anything but happy in ours.

The Yankee teams on which I played always hated defeat, especially in the important games. What made us feel so badly was that we realized we had licked ourselves. Everybody knew about the celebration old Aleck had attended that Saturday night, figuring he wouldn't be used again for the remainder of the Series. But not many knew that some of our own fellows had been out that same night—prematurely celebrating a Series victory that never came to us.

13

The Greatest Team in History

A man who has put away his baseball togs after an eventful life in the game must live on his memories, some good, some bad.

Of the good ones the one that stands out most of all is that of the greatest ball club that ever stepped onto a field, one that I played on and starred for—the 1927 Yankees.

We won 110 games that season, the American League record. We could do everything bigger and better than any club in the league and, as far as I'm concerned, any club ever brought together.

We had an individual champ in just about every position.

That was the year I hit 60 home runs, breaking my own record of 59—set in 1921—and establishing a mark that has not since been touched by the great sluggers who followed me in baseball.

We won the 1927 pennant from here to Christmas, and it wasn't a case of knocking over weak competition. There were a couple of clubs in the American League that year which could win pennants in either league today. The Philadelphia Athletics, for one. We beat them easily, though they were loaded with such players as Jimmie Foxx, Mickey Cochrane, Al Simmons, Ty Cobb (who hit .357 in that next-to-last year of his career), Lefty Grove and George Earnshaw.

We murdered the second division teams that year, especially the St. Louis Browns, managed that year by

Dan Howley, who once said he'd put a ring through my nose and tame me. We beat the Browns, 21 straight; and then, taking pity on them, we let them win the 22nd game, long after we had clinched the pennant.

Before the season started the club gave me another substantial raise. My five-year contract was up, and after my 1926 season I figured I deserved another raise. Ruppert was agreeable. But I made him blink and sputter when I asked for an $18,000 raise to $70,000.

"That's too high, 'Root,' " Jake said. "I agree that you're entitled to more money, but I hadn't thought of anything like that. I was thinking of an $8,000 raise, sending you up to $60,000. Why, any player would be overjoyed with an $8,000 increase, 'Root.' "

At a conference down in St. Petersburg he finally gave it to me. There was a wishing well down there, and he said, "I'm going to throw a coin in that well and wish you success for 1927. Throw one in yourself, Babe, and wish yourself a lot of luck." I did—and I had the luck.

By 1927 Huggins moved Gehrig ahead of Meusel in our batting order and Lou now batted fourth, immediately after me. He remained in that slot in the batting order for the remainder of his active career.

Lou and I broke up a lot of games that season. I drove in 164 runs, my second highest total; but that Dutchman topped me by driving in 175. I scored 158 runs to his 149. Our entire club scored 975 runs, and four men on the club, Lou, Meusel, Lazzeri and I all batted in better than 100 runs.

I don't think I ever would have established my home-run record of 60 if it hadn't been for Lou. He was really getting his beef behind the ball that season and finished with 47 home runs. At one time we were almost neck and neck, and the papers were carrying what they called the home-run barometer showing what Lou and I were doing up to the minute. Pitchers began pitching to me, because if they passed me they still had Lou to contend with.

Well, I liked the big kid and admired him; he had many likeable qualities. But it also was fun to kid the Dutchman by asking him what he ever had learned in Columbia. If he had beaten me out, it would have put a crimp in my kidding. So I really put the wood to the ball in September and eventually left him behind, finishing 13 home runs to the good.

Speaking of my 60 home runs in 1927, they were made before many of the parks had been artificially changed so as to favor the home-run hitter. I hit them into the same parks where only a decade before ten or twelve homers were good enough to win the title. They said they livened the ball up for me, and some of the writers called it the jack-rabbit ball. Well, if they put some of the jack in it around the 1927 period, they put the entire rabbit into it in 1947 and at the same time shortened a lot of fences. But my old record has held up.

We had great pitchers in 1927: Pennock, Hoyt, Ruether, Shawkey, Pipgras, and Shocker, though poor Urban already was suffering from weak spells. None of us, however, suspected that he'd be dead within a year.

Ed Barrow, always looking for a sleeper in the deck, came up with the pitcher of the year. He was an out-and-out steal. His name was Wilcy Moore, and Barrow pulled him out of a little league in Carolina for $2000. I don't know where Moore was when all the scouts were gumshoeing around those parts, because he was just about the best pitcher in our league in 1927. Hug used him mostly as a relief man, but he was just as good as a starter, winning 19 games and coming up with the best earned-run average in the league.

Wilcy was a farmer who had some cotton acres in

Oklahoma. He was a big, easygoing, good-natured guy and the lousiest hitter in baseball history. I took a look at him the first day he worked for us and laid him $300 to $100 he wouldn't get three hits all season. It looked like a cinch, but the double-crosser bore down through the last half of the season and finished with five hits.

Wilcy took the $300 and bought a pair of mules. He named one Babe and the other Ruth, which probably surprised both of them.

We won the 1927 World Series the day before it started. The Pirates were the other club, and the first two games were scheduled for Forbes Field. Naturally, we showed up a day early and worked out in the strange park—and we won the Series during that workout.

You see, the Pirates had held their own practice first, and then they had had a little pep meeting and started back to their homes and hotels.

But by the time they came out of their dressing room, to start away from the park, the Yankees were taking batting practice. Most of them had never seen us, so they draped themselves here and there in the empty stands and took a look. Manager Donie Bush should have insisted that they go right home.

The 1927 Pirates had some darn good ballplayers: the Waners, Pie Traynor, Glenn Wright, old Joe Harris and a good pitching staff. But you could actually hear them gulp while they watched us.

We really put on a show. Lou and I banged ball after ball into the right-field stands, and I finally knocked one out of the park in right center. Bob Meusel and Tony Lazzeri kept hammering balls into the left-field seats.

One by one, the Pirates got up and left the park. Some of them were shaking their heads when we last saw them.

We got off to a good start by winning the first one

in Pittsburgh by a score of 5 to 4, though Hoyt almost blew the game in the late innings and Hug had to rush in Wilcy Moore to save it for us.

George Pipgras then was only a kid pitcher on our club, but Hug took a chance on him in the second game and Pip came through fine, winning by a score of 6 to 2. We decided after that game that we'd be the first American League club ever to win four straight in the World Series.

Herb Pennock pitched the third game for us, and it was one of the prettiest pitching performances I saw in my long major league career. Herb almost got away with a perfect game. He retired the Pirates in order in the first seven innings and then got the first man in the eighth—22 consecutive batsmen.

Nobody was letting out a peep on the bench nor making any reference to Pennock's pitching for fear of putting a jinx on him. I rooted for that perfect game as much as if I were pitching it. But I guess it wasn't to be, for Pie Traynor finally slapped a single to left, and, later, Clyde Barnhart doubled to give Pittsburgh its only run.

After the spell was broken it didn't matter much, and Lloyd Waner reached Herb for a third hit in the ninth. I knew the fans were expecting something from me, too, so I hit little Mike Cvengros, who had been in our league with the White Sox, for a homer later in the game. We won it, 8 to 1.

Now we were sure we could make it four straight. Ruppert wasn't a club owner who played for big gate receipts in the World Series, and we knew that nothing would please him better than to have his team score a knockout.

Huggins was so pleased with Moore's relief pitching in the first game that he gave Wilcy a chance to wind it up for us. A pitcher with specs, Carmen Hill, was on the mound for the Pirates. I thought I put the game on ice for us when I rammed a homer into our right-field bleachers in the fifth inning with Combs on base. But our boys booted a couple of plays in the seventh inning, and the score was tied at 3 to 3 when we went into the ninth. And that was one of the craziest innings I ever was in.

By then a big Serb named John Miljus was pitching for the Pirates. He started off by walking Combs, and then Mark Koenig beat out a hit. Mark was our hottest hitter in the Series and batted .500.

While I was up, Miljus let go a wild pitch, putting runners on second and third. Donie Bush then ran out and ordered Miljus to pass me, filling the bases. A run would beat Pittsburgh anyway, and by having the bags filled they had a possible force play at every base.

Miljus had a lot of moxie that day. With the sacks loaded he struck out Gehrig and Meusel, two of the toughest men in baseball. But that still left Lazzeri. Miljus bore down on Tony with everything he had, but when one of his fast balls sailed high and went over catcher Johnny Gooch's head, Combs raced home with the winning run of the World Series.

The play generally was scored as a wild pitch for Miljus, but there were a lot of people who thought Gooch should have stopped the ball. As a former pitcher, I know we often are charged for wild pitches when we think the fault was the catcher's, not ours.

What a crazy bunch of guys we were when we reached our clubhouse! Everybody was singing, dancing, yelling his fool head off. Ruppert came into the clubhouse and was so happy he could hardly talk.

"Well, Jake," I yelled at him, "I guess this makes you feel better after the way we blew the 1926 Series on you."

"You're right, 'Root,' " Ruppert beamed. "I never was so happy in my life. The team was wonderful and you were great."

At the dinner of the New York Baseball Writers the following winter they gave me the plaque for being the Player of the Year. They didn't give it to me because I had hit 60 home runs and had helped the club to a four-straight World Series by hitting the only two home runs of the Series. They told me they were giving it to me because of the comeback I had made after my terrible season of 1925, when a lot of them figured, and wrote, that I was all washed up.

I always got a big kick out of these annual dinners of the New York writers. I was at the first one, back in 1924, and I have missed few since then. I recall the first one. They had a character there named Vince Barnett, who played the part of a tough waiter. He insulted everybody, including Ruppert and Judge Landis, and he finally got on me. He kept poking me in the chest and yelling, "Whoever told you you were a ballplayer?"

Well, he had me crazy. Rosy Ryan of the Giants and I chased him all over the room, and Rosy finally brought him down with a flying tackle. We were starting to beat him up when the writers who had hired Barnett for the gag called us off and told us it was all a rib.

Just when I had him by the neck.

14

My Top Series Average—.625

John McGraw once said, "No club that wins a pennant once is an outstanding club. One which bunches two pennants is a good club. But a team which can win three in a row really achieves greatness."

By McGraw's way of figuring, or anybody else's, we proved ourselves a great combination in 1928, by winning our third straight pennant and our second World Series in four straight games.

I don't think we were as good in 1928 as in 1927, especially in the Series—where we had to get along without Pennock and Combs. But we had to be pretty darn good to win the 1928 pennant.

Connie Mack's young club was fast becoming one of the best of them all. And the gamest. We took a 13½-game lead over them shortly after July 4th that year, but they came on so fast in the second half of the season that they actually passed us by half a game early in September.

But our ball club knew how to get off the floor and punch back. We were all banged up when the cocky A's came to the Stadium the second week of September for a four-game series that was sure to decide the pennant. But we were ready.

With 80,000 people in the stands, we beat the stuffing out of them in a double-header on the first day of the series. Pipgras shut them out in the first game, and Hoyt beat them in the second when Meusel hit a home run with the bases loaded. Then we made it three straight with Henry Johnson winning and me hitting a homer, but little Bishop K.O.ed Hoyt with a homer in the fourth game. So the Yanks headed West with a two-game lead and held it.

I hit 54 home runs that season, and my batting eye stayed right sharp through the World Series. I hit .625 in that 1928 Series, a mark that has never been topped in the 20 World Series that have come and gone since that day.

Our opponents in 1928 were the Cardinals, with some of the same ballplayers who had been on the Cardinal team of 1926 which beat us in seven games. Hornsby had gone by that time, and Bill McKechnie was managing the Red Birds. We all liked Bill, but we set out to knock him sky high, and we did. Sam Breadon, the Cardinal boss, got so sore when we beat his club in four straight games—our second straight year of doing that—that he fired McKechnie, though the Deacon had just given him a pennant.

We looked like survivors of a bus wreck in that 1928 Series. Pennock's arm was so sore that he could not be used at all. Combs was kept out with a broken finger. Tony Lazzeri's right shoulder was in such bad condition that he could hardly throw the ball to first and couldn't come close to taking his full cut at the ball while hitting. Joe Dugan's knee was bad again. I had a sprained ankle and a charley horse.

But we knocked them dead, and one of our victims was Grover Cleveland Alexander.

I started the wrecking job in the first game, which was played at the Stadium. I doubled to right, off Sherdel, and Bob Meusel hit a home run into the left-field stands to give Hoyt the first game, 4 to 1.

Pipgras pitched our second victory, as he had done in Pittsburgh the year before. And this time we sent old Aleck to the cleaners, winning easily by a score of 9 to 3.

Hug didn't have Pennock available, so he pitched

his remaining southpaw, Tom Zachary, in our first game in St. Louis. We coasted through this one, 7 to 3. I guess it would have been only 6 to 3 if I hadn't slid into the plate with all my 230 pounds behind it. Jimmy Wilson, the catcher, was waiting for me with a ball, but dropped it after the impact.

The fourth game was a great one for me. When I hit three home runs in one game in Sportsman's Park in the 1926 World Series, one of the writers wrote, "We've seen history made here today, a performance which probably never will be duplicated."

But I showed them that history repeats itself, because I again knocked three out of that park.

Hoyt and Sherdel, the opening-game pitchers, were at it again, and we were trailing, 2 to 1, in the seventh, our run resulting from my homer earlier in the game. There was one out in this seventh and Sherdel quickly got two strikes on me. I stepped back a moment, and as I did so he threw what they call a quick pitch right through the middle. The St. Louis crowd gave a loud yell of joy, thinking Sherdel had struck me out. But Umpire Pfirman, a National Leaguer, behind the plate, wouldn't allow the strike.

That stirred up the entire Cardinal bench. McKechnie, Frankie Frisch, Rabbit Maranville and Jimmy Wilson swarmed around Pfirman demanding to know why I wasn't out. Above the noise I could hear the umpire insist, "It wasn't a legal pitch."

McKechnie demanded that Pfirman call in the other umpires but they upheld Pfirman. The so-called quick pitch was allowed in the National League that year, but when Judge Landis gave instructions to the umpires he told them he did not want to see it used in the World Series.

The crowd couldn't understand it. They had seen the third strike come over and yelled murder when I stayed at the plate. They started to take it out on me. And one loudmouth in a front-row box yelled, "What are you standing up there for, you big bum? Don't you even know three strikes is out?"

That made me mad, and when Sherdel pitched again I drove the ball over the roof of the right-field stands, tying the score. That gave Lou Gehrig the same idea, and he followed with a smash to exactly the same spot. Alexander was brought on in the eighth and our thoughts went back to 1926 when "Ol' Pete" pulled his great relief job. But this time he didn't have a thing. I hit my third home run of the game, and we won it, 7 to 3.

In the ninth inning I also had the pleasure of winding up the game and the Series with a running catch of Jim Bottomley's ball, which I speared off the lap of a fan in one of the left-field boxes. I forgot all about my charley horse and my sore ankle as I sprinted after that ball. And I never stopped running after the catch. With the ball held high for all the fans to see, I dashed for the dugout.

Ruppert had a train waiting for us in the event that we won four straight. In fact, he said he never had any doubt about it. "My boys don't believe in letting these World Series drag out," he said.

They say baseball started in 1839, and there probably have been many thousands of trains carrying ballplayers since the game was invented. But I doubt if there ever was another train ride to match our wild ride out of St. Louis on the night of our great triumph. This wasn't a usual victory. When you win two straight World Series without the loss of a game it calls for something special.

By midnight we were as crazy as a bunch of wild Indians. We paraded through the entire train and everyone had to sacrifice his shirt, if he was still up, or his pajama coat, if he had gone to bed. Not only the ballplayers were in this victory jamboree, but I remember Ford Frick, my ghost writer, and Dick

Vidmer were right up at the head of the parade with Lou and myself.

Ruppert locked himself in his drawing room, but it was no go. He had another old geezer with him, a guy with a little goatee whom we used to call "Colonel" Wattenberg. He was about the same age as Colonel Jake. We knocked at their door, and Jake called out, "Go away; I've already turned in and want to get some sleep."

"This is no night for sleeping," I yelled through the door.

"Go away, 'Root,' " Jake said.

I gave Lou Gehrig a signal. We put our shoulders to the door and pushed right through the panel. I reached through, unlocked the door, and a moment later Lou, Pat Collins, several others and myself tumbled into the room. I got away with Jake's lavender pajama coat and Gehrig undressed Wattenberg, carrying off the top of his pajamas for a souvenir.

Little Huggins wasn't a drinking man. His digestion was bad and he couldn't stand hard liquor. But even he broke down on this night of nights, and the next morning he went through the train asking over and over again, "Did anybody see my teeth?"

Three young fellows who made a lot of baseball history were with the Yankees that season: two kid infielders, Leo Durocher and Ben Chapman, and a lanky kid catcher, Bill Dickey. Leo and Ben were with us at the St. Petersburg training camp in the spring. Hug retained Durocher as a utility player, but Ben was sent out for minor league seasoning.

All three of them went on to play in the World Series and won jobs as big league managers. And all had their troubles. Chapman was barred for a year as a minor league manager for attacking an umpire. Dickey ran afoul of the eccentric Larry MacPhail. Durocher met up with Commissioner Happy Chandler—and lost.

I've seen my share of fresh rookies. I was one my-self. But Durocher was the cockiest busher I ever saw. He didn't get that nickname of Lippy for nothing. He talked a blue streak from the first day he appeared in a Yankee uniform, and when he decided to ride somebody he didn't care how big the fellow was or how tough or how much better a ballplayer he was than Lippy.

Leo picked on Ty Cobb, for instance. Ty played his last baseball in 1928, with the A's, and to show you what kind of an eye the old guy still had—after 25 years of ballplaying—he hit .325.

Cobb got hold of a long one to right center one day, when we were trying Durocher at shortstop. The old Georgia Peach rounded first, then roared past second and headed for third.

But as he passed Leo, Lippy gave him the hip and knocked the tough old guy right on his kisser. We threw him out at third base by 20 feet.

Cobb wheeled on Durocher and started back at him and, remembering that Cobb had the most acid tongue in baseball and was always handy with his dukes, I figured that our fresh young shortstop finally was going to get his education.

Cobb cursed Leo for a long time and finally said, "If you ever do that to me again I'll cut your legs off."

That fresh Lippy laughed right in Cobb's face.

"Go home, Grandpa, you might get hurt playing with us young guys," he said.

I thought Cobb would explode. Nobody—certainly no rookie—had ever dared to talk to him like that. He started to say something else but Leo took charge again.

"And listen, Grandpa," he added, "you're not going to cut off anybody's legs. You've gotten away with murder for a lot of years, but you're through, see? I'll give you the hip every time you come around my way, and if you try to cut me I'll ram a ball right down your throat."

Cobb got dizzy with rage and started for Leo, but we broke it up. And one of the Yanks turned to me and said, "That busher's never going to shine anybody's shoes."

People who didn't know Leo sometiines mistook him for a dude. Barrow was checking over some spring-training laundry charges early in 1928 and thought there had been a mistake. The rookie Durocher's bill was twice that of Jake Ruppert, who was always a very fastidious fellow. Barrow ordered Leo to take it easy, but Leo ignored him.

One night at St. Pete our brash young man dressed up in an immaculate dinner jacket, hoisted a snappy cane he had bought and started from his room to a date he had.

But he figured he might run into me or Meusel or some other Yank who might rip his pretty coat up the back, just for a laugh, so he ducked out a side door of the Princess Martha Hotel. He thought he had made a perfect getaway when he was stopped by a voice.

"Mighty sharp, young man, mighty sharp."

It was Miller Huggins, who was sitting on one of St. Pete's famous green benches and watching Durocher's "escape."

"Hello, Mr. Huggins," Durocher said. "Just going out for dinner."

Hug looked him over.

"I hope you're handier with that cane than you are with a bat, Leo," Hug said.

Leo never was much of a hitter. I tried to help him once. I suggested that he become a switch hitter and that if he did his average would jump to .400. "Two hundred right-handed and two hundred left," I said.

My interest in kids kept sharpening until I reached the point where I got as much of a kick out of my association with them as they seemed to receive from their meetings with me. There was usually a sick boy who needed a visit, and these experiences were much alike: a crying voice on the telephone, a tear-streaked face in a hotel lobby, mumbled explanations.

Sometimes I just couldn't go, because if I had walked out on crowds that had bought tickets because I was to play, I would have been lynched. But at other times I'd get a break—an off day or a postponement.

For instance: during the spring of 1928 a man came up to me in a Knoxville hotel lobby. He had been crying. He begged me to drive out with him to his cabin—somewhere out in the hills—where he had a sick son. I told him I was awful sorry but I had to play ball that day and take a train, along with the rest of the Yankee team, as soon as the ball game was over.

It was hard to look at his face when I told him. But then I heard something. It was the sound of rain. I looked out and, to my complete surprise, it had started to rain. It came down in buckets, and I told the man to wait.

Finally, we got the word. The game had been called off. I looked at the man and said, "Come on, show me the way."

It took all day to get to the cabin and back to town. But the look on that kid's pale, sick face was enough of a reward for me.

I guess I was learning a few things, and among them was the meaning of friendship.

By 1928 Lou Gehrig and I were doing a lot of barnstorming together. That revolt by Bob Meusel and me in the fall of 1921 helped all ballplayers, especially those on championship teams. With some restrictions we were thereafter permitted to play until November 1st, and Christy Walsh billed Lou and me from one coast to the other.

Lou and I saw a lot of each other in those days, and I was a frequent visitor at the old Gehrig home in New Rochelle. We used to have some real good times up there. Bennie Bengough and Tony Lazerri also liked to go up there, and Mom Gehrig would try to cook enough pig's knuckles for all of us. She was a great cook and a real hostess, and Pop Gehrig liked to have Lou's gang eat with him. It was one of the rare tastes of home life I had ever had.

Once I brought a little Mexican hairless dog back from St. Louis and gave it to Mom Gehrig. She called it "Jidge," which was my special nickname on the ball club. Nobody calls me "Jidge" any more, but at one time the players in the clubhouse rarely called me anything else. "Jidge," the dog, was a sickly little pup and we often wondered whether it would live. If anyone at that time had suggested that "Jidge" would outlive the muscular, super-healthy Lou, he would have been considered crazy.

But "Jidge" did just that.

15

An Eventful Season

Many things happened to me in the season of 1929, the most important being my marriage on April 17th to my present wife, Claire Merritt Hodgson.

My first wife, Helen, met a tragic death earlier in the year when a fire consumed the Massachusetts house in which she lived. We had not been together for several years.

Claire has been a faithful wife, friend, counselor and pal through the years. She seldom left my side during my long hospitalization and convalescence during the winter of 1946–47. She did much to pull me through the roughest trip of a pretty rough life.

Claire had many things I did not possess: culture, background, good looks. She was born in Jefferson, Ga., but grew up in Athens, where her father, James Monroe Merritt, taught law at the University of Georgia. Claire chose a career on the stage.

I met Claire in Washington at a game at Griffith Stadium. She was appearing in a musical with Jimmy Barton, who is a first-class baseball fan. Claire invited me to see the show that night, but I brought along three or four other Yankees and the poor kid got stuck for the seats.

We were married by Father William F. Hughes at the Church of St. Gregory the Great in Manhattan. I was supposed to play a ball game that afternoon but we were rained out at the Stadium until the next day when we defeated the Red Sox, 7 to 3. As a sort of wedding present for Claire I hit a home run. Then Lou Gehrig gave us his present with another four-bagger. It is interesting to recall that the pitcher off whom we made these home runs was Red Ruffing, who was soon to come to the Yankees, where he starred for many years.

As usual, we trained for the 1929 season in St. Petersburg. By this time the town knew us well, and I guess I was as familiar a figure down there as Al Lang, their former mayor, who calls himself the "Ambassador of Sunshine."

Sammy Byrd, at present one of the top-notch golfers of the country, then was a Yankee rookie in his first training camp. Later the sports writers called Sammy "Babe Ruth's Legs," when I got along in years and would take myself out of the games in the late innings.

I learned that spring of 1929 that Sammy was one of the most natural golfers alive. It was several years before Sunday baseball came to St. Petersburg and on Sundays Miller used to let the gang out to play golf at the old Jungle Club. Mark Koenig and Mike Gazella were leaving the hotel for the Jungle when Byrd shyly asked whether he could go along. They thought it over, shrugged and said, "Okay, Kid, come along." Maybe they expected him to caddy.

In the clubhouse before they teed off, Mark and Mike explained to Sammy that they played for caddy fees and the cost of the lunch. They added that they wouldn't include Sammy because they were both good and didn't want to stick him.

Sammy knocked off a birdie on the second hole and then opened their eyes with an eagle three on a par five. Koenig and Gazella were low-80 shooters, but they never won a hole.

They rushed back to the hotel to steam me into a match with Byrd. That was easy, I had been the low handicap man on the ball club for several years. I felt

I could hit that pill a mile off the tee and was pretty proud of my short game.

"I'll take that busher," I yelled, and took all bets.

So they arranged for a match the following Sunday, and Byrd beat the pants off me. He turned out to be a first-class ballplayer, too, but his golf was so much better than his baseball that he became a pro and has done very well.

I worked a miracle that spring at Tampa. Shortly before game time an automobile drove onto the field and parked outside of the right-field foul line. We thought at first it was the mayor. But sitting on the front seat was a hunched-up kid with a grown man beside him.

When the game was over—we played and beat the Reds—we ran to our bus, which was parked on the old fair grounds. As I jogged past the parked car I looked at the wasted kid, waved and yelled, "Hi'ya, Kid."

I thought no more of it. But I learned later that my greeting had a remarkable effect on the boy. He rose up from his seat and called something back to me.

As Leo Durocher and Mrs. Lieb passed the car the boy's father had tears running down his cheeks. The man was overwhelmed. He kept repeating over and over again, "My boy stood up. My boy stood up. This is the first time in two years that my boy has stood up."

The Johnny Sylvester case has been written about a lot. I'm supposed to have helped cure Johnny, and then failed to recognize him later. Here's my story of the case, which happened at the close of the 1926 season.

So many crackpots used to call me up at the Stadium that I seldom accepted a call there unless I recognized the name of the caller. But I took the call that concerned Johnny, because whoever picked up the phone and took the message said it was about a kid—and it was urgent.

The man on the other end of the wire was Johnny's father. He told me that the boy had been in bed for a long time with a back ailment that had stumped the doctors. The croakers had done everything they could for him and they had finally told the father that the boy needed some kind of emtional jolt, some great stimulation. It might lift him out of his condition, the doctors said.

So the old man thought of me. He thought of me because the kid was a terrific fan of mine. The kid had saved my box scores and stories about me and pasted them in a scrapbook.

Would I send the kid a letter or—if possible—an autographed baseball, Johnny's father wanted to know.

"Where's the kid?" I asked the man.

"He's out here in Essex Fells, N. J.," the voice answered.

"Where the hell is that?" I asked.

He gave me the instructions.

"I'll be out this afternoon," I said.

"But the World Series starts tomorrow—" the man began. He seemed surprised I'd come.

"So I've got a day off today," I said.

They didn't tell the kid I was going to walk in on him, and I guess it must have been pretty much of a shock to him at that. I thought his eyes would pop out of his head.

I sat on his bed, gave him a glove, bat and ball I had brought along with me, told him he had to get up off his back and play ball just like other kids, and asked what else I could do for him.

He swallowed and asked me if I could hit a home run for him in the World Series which was about to open with the Cardinals.

I said sure, rubbed his head for luck and started back to New York.

I hit four home runs in that Series. I had no way of knowing it, but the kid improved not only from the hour of my visit but each home run seemed to give him new strength. They were "his."

About that time, some jerk said in print—or on the air—that my only interest in visiting sick kids and trying to cheer them up was for the publicity I got out of it. It seemed so damned unfair to me that I asked the writing boys after that to stay away from trips I took to see kids; to keep from tipping off the cameramen, and to stop writing about me in that connection.

I saw a lot of boys after I took that trip to Essex Fells to see Johnny Sylvester. And I had seen a lot before. I spent a fair portion of every day, during the summer, signing my way through a mob of kids before and after a ball game. I guess I've had as much direct contact with kids as any American who ever lived.

But I still get kidded for forgetting Sylvester's name. The following season, after my visit to Essex Fells, a man came up to me in a Philadelphia hotel lobby— one of, I might say, quite a few who used to do that.

"I'm Johnny Sylvester's uncle," he said.

"That so? How's Johnny?"

"It's a miracle, Mr. Ruth," the man said. "A miracle. We can never thank you enough for what you did for Johnny."

"Forget it," I said. "Give him my regards."

We shook hands and he left. And when he was out of earshot I turned to a couple of sports writers I had been talking to and said, "Who the hell is Johnny Sylvester?"

When they stopped laughing they told me, and, of course, I remembered right away.

Through the years, I lost track of almost all the kids I made a point of calling on during my long stay in the game. But Johnny and I have kept in touch with each other for a long time. Johnny grew up to be a fine, strapping lad and served as a submariner in the Navy during the war.

He was one of the few callers I was able to have in the weeks that followed my release from the hospital. And I needed his rooting as much as he once had needed mine.

But to go back to 1929.

The Yanks stumbled that year, tripped not only by the full bloom of Connie Mack's great Athletics but also by our own injuries and troubles.

Mark Koenig's eyes went bad and Hug put Durocher at short and tried to plug up our weakness at third base by bringing Lyn Lary in from the Coast League.

Durocher quickly earned his title as the "All American Out." But Lary showed signs of becoming a very good player. They were just signs. This is no reflection on either Leo or Lyn. They just happened to symbolize the decline of the Yankees from their great peak of 1927.

The A's ran us ragged in 1929. We kept up with them for half the season, and then they ran away from us as if we were cemented. We were a poor second.

I had some leg trouble that year and could play in only 135 games. But it was a good season for me. I hit .345, knocked out 46 home runs and batted in 154 runs.

It wasn't enough to hold off the A's. Shortly after Labor Day of 1929 we officially lost the pennant—and all hope of winning four of them in a row.

But that was a minor loss.

For we lost Miller Huggins.

Most of us saw the little guy alive for the last time on September 20th of that year. It had been a rough season for Hug. He had set his heart on becoming the first American League manager to pilot his club to four straight pennants, and our losing to the A's was a blow to him.

I had noticed as the season advanced that Hug's eyes began to sink back in his head. He never was much of an eater, but now he didn't eat enough to keep a canary alive. He seemed to shrink even smaller than he normally was.

We tried to cheer him up. I told him he'd snap out of it as soon as he got to St. Pete and lapped up some of that sunshine and golf. Art Fletcher, our coach, was a little more practical. He kept after Hug to see a doctor about the sore he was developing under one of his eyes.

"Go to a doctor because I've got a red spot on my face?" Hug demanded. "Me?—who took the spikes of Frank Chance and Fred Clarke?"

But Hug felt so bad after he walked home from the game on September 20th that he did permit a doctor to call on him at his apartment not far from the Stadium.

The sore was first diagnosed as a carbuncle, but it soon developed that Hug's whole system was full of poison. Yet his death, on September 25th, was one of the greatest shocks of my life. He was only 49.

We were a hard-boiled bunch, at least on the ball field. Most of us had had our scraps with Hug. We had cursed him when he tried to harness our energies, and he had cursed us. We had scrapped, but we had played for him; played up to the hilt for him.

There wasn't a dry eye at his funeral, at the Little Church Around the Corner, in downtown Manhattan. Big Lou, Tony, Waite, Earle and I knelt there and cried when the minister spoke his last words.

A few of us, and some of the regular baseball writers who knew Hug well, accompanied the body to its final resting place in Woodlawn Cemetery in Cincinnati. And for years after that, a delegation of the old

New York writers made a pilgrimage to Woodlawn each year to place a wreath on Hug's grave.

Art Fletcher took charge of us for the remaining days of the 1929 season, and we naturally assumed he'd be named manager. He knew the players and he knew baseball, for he had been captain of McGraw's teams and had managed the Phillies before taking a coaching job under Hug.

But when the job was offered to him Fletcher turned it down. Jake Ruppert couldn't believe his ears. Turning down a chance to manage the Yankees was—to Jake—like someone turning down a chance to be President.

Yet there it was. Fletch asked only that he be retained as a coach.

I was reading a paper one morning after the close of the season and the writer was speculating on who'd be manager of the Yanks now that Fletch had rejected the job.

There was a long plug for Eddie Collins, and one for Donie Bush, who had managed Washington in 1923 and the Pirates in 1927 when we beat them four straight in the Series.

Suddenly I looked up and said out loud, "Hey, what's the matter with *me?*"

I had been with the Yankee organization ten years; had been around the majors for 16 years; knew baseball.

I had seen some of the other stars of my time move on to managerial jobs—Cobb, Speaker, Collins, Sisler, Schalk, Bucky Harris, Hornsby and Dave Bancroft. Because of my pitching career, and my occasional work at first base as well as in the outfield, I felt I had a better knowledge of the game than almost any of them.

All of a sudden I was red-hot for that Yankee job. Huggins had always seemed so permanent to me that

I guess I never got around much to the standard day-dream of the big leaguer: to be a manager.

But now Hug was gone; they were looking for a new manager for "The House that Ruth Built," and what was wrong with me?

I soon found out.

But before I did I rushed over to Ruppert's office in the brewery and laid my cards on the table. I told him that I knew how to handle young pitchers—because I had been one myself; and I knew how to handle hitters—because I was one myself. I told him everything I could think of, but when I had finished he just shook his head, kind of sadly.

"You can't manage yourself, 'Root,' " he said. "How do you expect to manage others?"

I even had an answer for that.

"Listen, Colonel, I've been through the mill. I know every temptation that can come to any kid, and I know how to spot it in advance. And if I didn't know how to handle myself, I wouldn't be in baseball today."

I made my plea as strong as I could, and, to my joy, Ruppert seemed to melt.

"I know you're sincere about this, 'Root,' " he said. "Let me think it over for a day or two. Then I'll be in touch with you."

I waited a few days and was on the point of calling him again when I picked up a newspaper and a head-line hit me in the eye. It read:

BOB SHAWKEY NAMED YANKEE MANAGER

16

Eighty Thousand a Year

It wasn't that I had anything against Shawkey. Bob and I hit it off great from the day I first met him, and we're still great friends. But I felt I should have been given the job of managing the 1930 Yankees.

When I got over my first disappointment, I decided to do two things. I got in touch with Bob to congratulate him and to promise him I'd give him the best that was in me. And, secondly, I decided that I'd get more money out of the Yankee front office. I give Shawkey an "assist" on that determination.

I had been paid at the rate of $70,000 a year for the previous three seasons. My contract was up and, as is the custom of most ball clubs, they sent me another contract calling for the same money.

I sent it back, and pretty soon I was closeted with Jake Ruppert. Most of the players dickered with Ed Barrow, but I had always done business with Ruppert himself. It wasn't just a case of going over Ed's head. He liked the idea as much as I did. He had found out, earlier, that Ruppert usually got around to paying me almost as much as I asked for—and more than Barrow himself would agree to pay, if left on his own— so he turned me over to Ruppert to save time and trouble.

"You don't like your contract, 'Root'?" Ruppert asked me as I sat down. He was wearing his stern, businesslike face.

"No, I don't," I said. "I know it s a lot of money

but it isn't what I'm worth." I meant that and still believe it. Few ballplayers can point definitely to certain attendance figures and claim them as his own. It so happened that I could. Once, in Chicago, I came down sick and when it was announced in the papers two days before the scheduled appearance of the Yankees there on a Sunday, there were more than 15,000 cancellations of ticket orders.

The Yanks used me in every exhibition game, and scheduled as many of these as they could crowd into their season's open dates. I don't think I had two or three days off during my whole stay with the Yanks. They made a lot of those one-day stands.

I think this constant pressure shortened my playing life by a year or two, but that's beside the point now. What I'm saying here—and what I told Jake Ruppert that day in 1930—is that I wasn't being paid in proportion to the number of people I was drawing. And I wasn't.

"What do you want?" Ruppert asked.

"A hundred thousand dollars a year," I said. If I blinked an eye I don't remember it, but Ruppert sure did. You would have thought I asked for his brewery.

Ruppert said that I must be out of my mind, and wouldn't speak further about the contract that day. But we saw each other several times that winter, before the club went South to St. Pete, and by the time I left with the team—unsigned—Jake had reluctantly offered me $80,000, plus the return of the $5000 fine which had been slapped on me in 1925.

It isn't customary for a player to work out when he is not under contract, but I trained faithfully with the Yankees up to the time that we were scheduled for our first exhibition game against the Braves.

There was some question whether I would play in this contest. Al Lang, the skinny old gent who runs baseball in St. Pete, was running around in circles. They had advertised me. I suppose in a feeling of good will I agreed to play in the game, even though I was not under contract.

There have been a lot of stories as to how I finally came to sign for $80,000 before that exhibition game. Claire and I were not staying with the club at their hotel in town. We had an apartment out at the Jungle Club. On the morning of the Braves game, Frick, my ghost writer, and Alan Gould, sports editor of the Associated Press, came out to see me.

We gabbed a bit and then Frick said, "Suppose you get hurt in that game, Babe. You'll be up against it in your contract fight."

"Hell, I never thought of that," I replied.

Well, the upshot of it was that they asked me what Ruppert's last offer was and I told them $80,000. Frick and Gould both said that was a lot of money, and suddenly I decided I'd better take it and sign a contract before playing in the afternoon game.

Gould had hired a little jalopy, and I got in it and we drove into town to the Princess Martha Hotel, where the Colonel was stopping. When we arrived we learned that Ruppert was out taking a walk with his pal, Wattenberg, and his secretary, Al Brennan.

We enlisted the aid of some baseball writers and they finally rounded up Jake. I signed for two years at $80,000 a year, and when the little ceremony was over Ruppert said, "Now, Babe, you are getting more money than the President of the United States."

"What about the fine?" I asked him. It had always been a sore subject with me.

Ruppert turned helplessly to Barrow.

"If it's up to me," Ed said, "the fine will have to remain."

"You promised it to me," I said to Ruppert.

Ruppert called Barrow aside and they had a few whispered words. Then Jake said, "So long as Huggins was alive, 'Root,' I'd never have given it back. It had to stand for Miller's sake. But he's dead now and he'll never know about this, and if it will please you we will give you back that five thousand."

I often have been asked whether my holdout battles with Jake were on the level. A good many fans, as well as my friends, got the idea they were staged for ballyhoo purposes, for they usually came just before or during the training season. There never was anything phony about them. Of course, we remained friends through them, even though occasionally we passed some sharp words. The only time I was really sore was when Ruppert gave out the salary we agreed upon to one of the reporters before I signed, which enabled him to scoop a lot of the other fellows that I was most friendly with.

We finished third for Shawkey in 1930, when the Athletics won for the second straight year and the Senators, under Walter Johnson, finished second. With the exception of that horrible season in 1925, third was our poorest finishing position since we started winning pennants in 1921.

We all played hard for Bob, but it was just one of those years. Personally, I hit .359, knocked out 49 homers, scored 150 runs, and drove in 153. Gehrig hit .379 just a shade behind league-leading Al Simmons, hit 41 homers and drove in 174.

Late in the season there were rumors in the New York papers that Bob Shawkey would not be retained. Ruppert was the kind of owner who thought finishing third was a personal insult.

When Bob was officially released, I again went to see Ruppert and made a second bid for the Yankee managerial job. Jake was ready for me. He recited a long list of my early mistakes—he had had somebody look them up—and at the end he shrugged.

"Under those circumstances, 'Root,' how can I turn my team over to you?"

I asked him whether there was any fault with my

conduct in 1930 or my efforts to make Shawkey's year a success.

"No, 'Root,' you really earned the big money that I paid you," he said. But as for the open managerial post, this time he did not even promise to "let me know."

Four days before the close of the 1930 National League season the Cubs let out Joe McCarthy, who had won the 1929 championship and was regarded as a smart manager in the other league. Joe's 1930 club had a lot of power. Hack Wilson set a National League home-run record with 56 and a runs-batted-in record of 190, which still stands. However, the club flopped in the closing weeks of the race and a red-hot Cardinal club beat them for the pennant. I guess that made Phil Wrigley, the Chicago owner, sore. He released Joe and put Rogers Hornsby, the old St. Louis manager, in charge.

If McCarthy had not suddenly become available, through being fired, I might have had a chance to succeed Shawkey. But again they weren't looking my way when they made their selection, and McCarthy was named about a week after the end of the Series. I knew my chances had been slim, but it still hurt.

I believe it was Ed Barrow more than Ruppert who prevented me from stepping into the Yankee managerial office. I am sure it was Ed who sold Ruppert on the idea of engaging McCarthy and vetoing my managerial bid. I don't think Ed realized that I had matured, was finally a grown man with family responsibilities and not the pipe-smoking playboy he had pulled the covers off in that hotel room in 1919.

I worked under McCarthy on the Yankees for the next four seasons. During that time there never was any intimacy between us. I played for him two hours or more in the afternoon; then our paths rarely crossed. At the start, some of our players didn't like Joe. They felt I was entitled to the job, and there was what might be called an anti-McCarthy faction on the club early in 1931.

One of the first things Joe did when we opened the season in New York was to smash a little card table we had in the clubhouse.

"This is a clubhouse, not a clubroom, and I want players in here to think of baseball and nothing else," he announced.

Joe was right. But we could have told him that the Yankee teams of 1926, 1927, and 1928 had done pretty well at baseball, even though we occasionally had a little game in the clubhouse before or after ball games.

I'll say this for McCarthy: In one of his first speeches to us he suddenly sounded like a Yankee—and a top one.

"I'm no second division manager and I won't stand for second division baseball," he barked. He meant it, too, as his later record showed.

McCarthy was anxious to improve the club's position in his first season in charge, and I know I helped bat him into second place with a strong September finish. I hit .373 for him, which was my highest average since I won the batting championship in 1924. I also knocked out 46 home runs and drove in 163 runs, the third highest of my career. I closed the season with 199 hits.

After trying to pass me in home runs ever since 1927, Lou Gehrig finally tied me with his 46 in 1931. Christy Walsh was as pleased as Lou. He wanted us to keep up this struggle on the exhibition belt after the season, and even had literature and letterheads printed about Lou and I still battling it out for the home-run crown through the provinces. However, Gehrig signed a contract with Fred Lieb to go on a trip to Japan at the end of the season and I did my barnstorming alone.

The Japanese newspaper sponsoring the trip, *Yomuiri Shimbun* of Tokyo, was also most anxious that I make the trip, and Lieb hounded me for a good part of the season trying to get me to go along. But Walsh had signed me to a contract to do some movie shorts in Hollywood after my barnstorming trip, and I had to pass it up.

The Japanese newspapers got themselves out on a limb by announcing that I would make the trip, and in September they offered me $25,000 if I would accompany the team of American baseball stars. When I had to turn that down they cabled Lieb, "Sign Ruth no matter what you have to pay him." Something they called "face" was at stake. He showed me the cablegram, but again I reluctantly told him my movie commitments would prevent me from accepting this fine offer. But I heard much of Japanese baseball and was curious to see how they played the game over there. I decided that I would make the trip at the first opportunity.

I had no way of knowing that not many years later, near the end of a savage war with Japan, I'd be considered as a United States peace emissary.

17

Ten Series—And Out

In 1932 I played on my tenth and last pennant winner and in my tenth World Series. During their terms as players and coaches, Art Fletcher and Earle Combs participated in more Series, and Frankie Frisch played in a greater number of games. But I am the only player who actually got into the box scores of ten of these fall championships.

I had to take a $5000 cut in 1932. We then were up to our armpits in the Depression. Ball clubs were cutting expenses right and left. The leagues knocked Judge Landis down from $65,000 to $50,000, reduced the pay of the league presidents and umpires, and other players had to take cuts. So I certainly had no kick coming when I signed for $75,000.

Joe McCarthy got us clicking early in the 1932 season and no one got ahead of us. It was a year before Connie Mack broke up his great team; but the old Philadelphia champions weren't in our class that year, and after midseason we were never pressed. In fact we won 107 games, only three less than our almost unbeatable team of 1927.

The team had undergone considerable changes since we won our last pennant and Series four years before. Hoyt and Koenig had been traded to the Tigers in Shawkey's year. Waite then played with half a dozen clubs, while Mark fell back to the minors, only to make a strong comeback with the Cubs' 1932 National League champions. Dugan's knee finally buckled up on him and he passed out of the big leagues after a brief period with the Braves. Meusel and Durocher were both sold to the Cincinnati Reds.

But Gehrig, Lazzeri, Combs, Pipgras, Pennock and I remained from the old champions. Frankie Crosetti an expensive Coast leaguer, was our new shortstop, and McCarthy plugged his third base hole by getting Joe Sewell from Cleveland.

Joe was the little collegian who filled in at shortstop for Cleveland after Ray Chapman was killed in 1920. He was a smart hitter and one of the toughest men to strike out I've ever seen in baseball. Joe wouldn't strike out more than two or three times a season.

In left field, in place of Bob Meusel, we now had the hard-running Ben Chapman. Ben first came to us as an infielder, but after we had so many outfield injuries early in the 1931 season that McCarthy had to play pitcher Ruffing in right field, Joe finally converted Ben into an outfielder. Ben stayed out there as long as he remained in the league.

Pennock, who came into the league two years before me, was used mainly in relief, but we had two new pitching aces in Red Ruffing and Lefty Gomez. Barrow bought Ruffing from Boston. Red couldn't win up there, but once he got the Yankee power boys in back of him he became a consistent 20-game winner and was almost unbeatable in the World Series.

Gomez first came to us in 1930, Shawkey's year, but he wasn't quite ready and Bob sent him to St. Paul to ripen. He was a tall, skinny, good-natured kid, and when we first saw him at St. Petersburg we wondered how such a skinful of bones could have so much stuff.

The Yankees bought Lefty from the San Francisco club for $40,000, and he was a great bargain at that price. The club's first problem was to try to fatten him up, and in the winter of 1930–31 they turned him loose with a herd of cows out in California and told him to drink all the milk he could absorb. He drank a ton of it and gained two pounds. "Nobody can fatten up a greyhound," he told us when he showed up at spring training.

Lefty was one of the few good ones who could laugh, gab with the crowd, watch the airplanes sail over and have a good time and a lot of laughs and still turn in a good performance. He was grand company and a grand fellow.

We had another fine young pitcher with us in 1932, but his personality was the reverse of Lefty's. He was a hotheaded young Southerner named Johnny Allen, with a world of stuff. His early boyhood was similar to mine, for he was a product of an orphanage in North Carolina. Johnny was a fighter. He'd fight the other side, the umpires, his own team and also, quite frequently, himself. But he contributed heavily to our 1932 pennant.

In the meantime, Bill Dickey had come along as a catcher since he joined us in the last weeks of 1928. He caught over 125 games each season, was a hard and dangerous hitter, and he began making fans hesitate before they said what they had been saying for some time—that Mickey Cochrane was the league's best catcher.

We were winning so easily that we were a carefree club around Labor Day. The straw hat season supposedly ends in New York on September 15th. But it used to end on Labor Day for the Yankees. If anybody wore one of those straw kelleys after that holiday it was just too bad.

We were coming back from a trip and Charlie Segar, then of the New York *Mirror* and now National League publicity man, knew I was on the prowl after his expensive Panama hat. Charlie gave the porter two-bits to hide the hat from me; but I gave him a buck to disclose the hiding place. When old Seg tip-toed to the hiding place of the hat, at the end of the trip, he found the benny in 50 pieces, and innocent looks on all of our faces.

If there was a certain tension between Joe McCarthy and me it certainly didn't affect our having a grand 1932 World Series. I don't know which of us got a bigger kick out of it.

For the third time we cleaned up the National Leaguers in four straight games, giving us the unbelievable record of 12 consecutive World Series victories over three different teams. The reason it was such a kick for Joe, naturally, was that Wrigley had booted him on the charge that Joe wasn't the type of manager who could bring him a world's championship.

I had a good Series, hit .333 and two home runs, including one that's part of the history of baseball. But I'll hand it to the big Dutchman, Gehrig. Lou was the solid man of the 1932 Series. In the four games he hit .529, got nine hits, three of them homers, scored nine runs and drove in eight.

We started off in the Stadium and easily won our games by scores of 12 to 6 and 5 to 2. Maybe I did let a few get by me on a wet field in the first game; but I had three runs and one hit in three official times at bat. Gehrig busted one, and we gave Guy Bush an awful shellacking. Ruffing was our winner.

Gomez then landed his first World Series victory when he won a 5 to 2 decision over Lon Warneke in the second game.

We moved to Chicago, where Claire and I were given a reception we'll never forget.

There was a lot of ill-feeling between the two clubs by this time, and I don't mind saying I had much to do with it. I have already said that Mark Koenig, our old Yankee shortstop contributed much to the Chicago pennant after the Cubs procured him in August. Without Mark's inspired play I don't believe the Chicago club, by this time managed by Charlie Grimm, could have won. But the Cubs went mercenary and voted Koenig only a half share in the World Series. Hornsby, who had managed the club until early August, wasn't given anything.

As soon as the Cubs came on the field for the first game in New York I yelled at them, "Hey, you lousy bunch of cheapskates!" To Mark I yelled, "Why do you associate with a bunch of bums like that, Mark?" Lazzeri, a sharp-tongued needler, took up the same plaint, as did Gehrig, Combs and some of our other boys. We called them nickel-nursers and misers, and, of course, they came back at us as best they could. They rode me about having wanted to manage the Yankees, called me grandpop, and wondered how long my old legs would hold up.

The Chicago writers made a lot of the feud and by the time the Yanks got to Chicago for the Wrigley Field portion of the Series, the Chicago fans were in a lather.

Especially the lady fans. The Cubs had gone in very strongly for ladies' days that season, and had made a lot of fanatics out of the otherwise orderly housewives of Chicago. I've seen some nutty fans in my life, but never any quite like those gals. Their darling boys on the Cubs could do no wrong, and my insults to those players—having been publicized in the Chicago papers—became insults to the ladies themselves.

When Claire and I reached the Edgewater Beach Hotel on the North Side of Chicago we were forced to run a gauntlet of two lines of hysterical, angry women. Most of their wrath was directed against me, and during that rough trip to the front door I heard some words that even I had never heard before.

But what annoyed me was their spitting; their spitting and their bad aim. Poor Claire received most of it—in what was practically her introduction to the fans.

I was so hopping mad by the time we got to our suite upstairs that I told Claire I'd fix them, somehow.

"I'll belt one where it hurts them the most," I said, without knowing just what I'd do—or how.

I guess it was while I was angry that the idea of "calling my shot" came to me. It wasn't exactly a new idea with me. I had hit a few home runs after promising to hit them, and in most of those cases I had been able to pick the very spot.

For instance, back in my early days with the Yanks, when we still played at the Polo Grounds, I teed off on one late in a tight ball game. The ball went up into the lower right-field stands and hit a tall iron girder down the middle of which ran a white foul line.

I started to trot toward first base, but Billy Evans, umpiring behind the plate, called me back by yelling "Foul!"

I came back and walked up to him. "What was wrong with that?" I asked him, waving my arms and throwing my cap down to indicate to the fans that I was madder than I really was.

"It was an inch to the foul side of the line," Billy said.

"Okay," I said, stepping back into the batting box, "watch this one. It will be an inch fair."

I hit the next pitch almost exactly as I hit the first one. It went on a line into the stands and hit the same upright girder. I looked around at Billy.

"It was an inch fair," Billy said. "Go ahead."

I've already spoken of those homers-on-order for Johnny Sylvester. I hit another one about that time for Mark Roth, our traveling secretary, when I noticed him biting his fingers in the grandstand, while we went into the 13th inning of a game.

Walking over to Roth I asked him what was eating him. It seems he was holding a train for us, to beat it out of town after the game, and the railroad was griping.

"Why didn't you say so earlier," I asked him. "I'll

take care of it." The pitcher threw me one that looked fat and I broke up the game.

There was a funny one in 1928, too. The Yanks were playing an exhibition game in Fort Wayne, Ind., and one of the first fans to show up at the ball park was the father of Ford Frick. He thought Ford might be traveling with us, but Ford had made other arrangements. So I fixed old man Frick up with a seat in a box behind the Yankee dugout. Even got him a cushion, for he was in his 70's then and mighty brittle-looking.

Fort Wayne gave us a lot of trouble that day. At the end of eight innings we were still tied up, and as I walked toward the plate I took a look at Mr. Frick. He looked very tired.

"I'll end it for you, Pappy," I called to him, "so you can trot home and get your nap." In the distance a long train of open cars was passing.

"See those cars, Pappy?" I yelled above the noise. "Watch."

I hit one over the right-field fence and into one of the cars—which may still be traveling, for all I know.

Frick's dad died in November, 1947, at the wonderfully ripe age of 95. Ford, now President of the National League, was never able to convince the fine old fellow that I couldn't hit home runs whenever I felt like it.

Some of these memories came back to me as I made up my mind to do something about the Cubs, and Cub fans in general, in that hotel suite in Chicago in 1932.

The Yanks and Cubs were two of the sorest ball clubs ever seen when they took the field for the third game, with George Pipgras pitching for us and Charley Root throwing for them.

But no member of either team was sorer than I was. I had seen nothing my first time at bat that came close to looking good to me, and that only made me more determined to do something about taking the wind out of the sails of the Chicago players and their fans. I mean the fans who had spit on Claire.

I came up in the fourth inning with Earle Combs on base ahead of me. My ears had been blistered so much before in my baseball career that I thought they had lost all feeling. But the blast that was turned on me by Cub players and some of the fans penetrated and cut deep. Some of the fans started throwing vegetables and fruit at me.

I stepped back out of the box, then stepped in. And while Root was getting ready to throw his first pitch, I pointed to the bleachers which rise out of deep center field.

Root threw one right across the gut of the plate and I let it go. But before the umpire could call it a strike—which it was—I raised my right hand, stuck out one finger and yelled, "Strike one!"

The razzing was stepped up a notch.

Root got set and threw again—another hard one through the middle. And once again I stepped back and held up my right hand and bawled, "Strike two!" It was.

You should have heard those fans then. As for the Cub players they came out on the steps of their dugout and really let me have it.

I guess the smart thing for Charley to have done on his third pitch would have been to waste one.

But he didn't, and for that I've sometimes thanked God.

While he was making up his mind to pitch to me I stepped back again and pointed my finger at those bleachers, which only caused the mob to howl that much more at me.

Root threw me a fast ball. If I had let it go, it would have been called a strike. But this was *it*. I swung from the ground with everything I had and as I hit the ball every muscle in my system, every sense I had, told me that I had never hit a better one, that as long as I lived nothing would ever feel as good as this.

I didn't have to look. But I did. That ball just went on and on and on and hit far up in the center-field bleachers in exactly the spot I had pointed to.

To me, it was the funniest, proudest moment I had ever had in baseball. I jogged down toward first base, rounded it, looked back at the Cub bench and suddenly got convulsed with laughter.

You should have seen those Cubs. As Combs said later, "There they were—all out on the top step and yelling their brains out—and then you connected and they watched it and then fell back as if they were being machine-gunned."

That home run—the most famous one I ever hit—did us some good. It was worth two runs, and we won that ball game, 7 to 5.

We didn't let the Cubs or their fans suffer too long. We knocked them dead the next day in the fourth and final game, 13 to 6. But it wasn't quite as easy as that. They got off to a big early lead when Demaree hit Johnny Allen, our starting pitcher, for a three-run home run.

But we soon got those back, and lots more. Gehrig and I didn't do too much about overcoming the Cub lead. But Lazzeri and Combs hit three homers between them, with Tony getting two, and we simply rode home.

The trip back to New York was about as wild as any of these returns, but it wasn't up to the 1928 party. Ruppert beamed and strutted all over the train, telling everybody he had the greatest team in the world. And you can imagine how happy McCarthy was after winning this clean sweep over the club that had given him the tramp's toss. Ruppert got back to New York with his pajama coat intact. Maybe we were getting older. Or maybe *I* was.

That year of 1932 was a pretty good one for all

concerned. One of my greatest thrills, I think, was watching Gehrig the day he "came of age," as one fellow wrote. On June 3rd Lou hit four home runs in a game at Shibe Park, Philadelphia. Only three other players in baseball history ever did that—Bobby Lowe, of the old Boston National League team, in 1894; Ed Delahanty, of the 1896 Philadelphia National; and Chuck Klein, of the Phillies, four years after Lou.

Lou should stand alone in that department. He should have had five that day. He got a fifth time at bat in the ninth inning of the game and hit his longest ball of the day. But Al Simmons dragged it out of the air near the center-field flagpole.

That's baseball.

18

The Rocking Chair Beckons

In 1933 I was back to the $52,000 salary I drew for my five Yankee seasons from 1921 to 1925. I didn't squawk too much about the cut, even though, for an old guy, I didn't do badly in 1932. I did miss 21 games; but when I was in there I still was walloping them to the fences. I batted .341 and had enough heft to jolt 41 home runs. My 120 runs and 137 runs batted in that year weren't bad, but I had done better.

The old legs were getting tired. I just couldn't get over the ground as well as I had only a few years before. McCarthy was sending in pinch-runners Byrd and Myril Hoag for me, and when we got ahead Joe would send one of these kid outfielders to right field in the late innings.

We had another young outfielder about this time named Dixie Walker, and some of the writers wrote that he would be my eventual successor. Oddly enough, Dixie then was a very brittle fellow. He was always hurting his knee, shoulder or something else. He hit smartly, but the writers used to kid him and say he was stuck together with chewing gum and picture-frame wire. We never thought he'd last more than half a dozen years. Yet he was a star outfielder on the Brooklyn National League Champions of 1947 some 14 years after we expected him to come apart at the seams.

Ruppert and Barrow gave the Depression, and the

fact that I was slowing up and had missed a number of games, as the reasons for my cut.

"Times are tough, Babe, and we can't pay out more money than comes in," Ruppert told me. He nearly had me in tears.

It was the winter when the country hit its low and Roosevelt closed the banks shortly after he followed Hoover into the White House. It was plainly no time to argue so I took the $52,000.

My 1933 season was pretty much the same as that of 1932. I did play in five more games, but my batting average dropped to .301. I drove in 103 runs and hit 34 homers. I just managed to stay ahead of the Dutchman. Lou had a good chance of beating me out that year, but finished with 33.

After our comparatively easy pennant victory in 1932, and clean sweep in the Would Series, the Yankees again were picked to win in 1933. It looked like smooth sailing when we went past Decoration Day with a .700 average. Then our pitchers began to go to pot and I wasn't far behind. It was our 1924 flop all over again.

In 1933 Washington was in charge of a new boy wonder, this time Joe Cronin, who was only 26—a fact which made me scratch my head and wonder if I'd ever be mature enough to become a manager. At first we paid no attention to the Senators, but the next thing we knew they had taken a little lead on July 4th and were getting tough with us in our own ball park.

It was a good, scrappy year. We staged two rhubarbs in Washington, once when Lou hit a home run—fair by inches—over Griffith Stadium's high right-field wall. It stayed a home run even though the Washington players and fans screamed bloody murder and Earl Whitehill, the Washington pitcher, threw Bick Owens' whisk broom over the grandstand roof.

We had what amounted to a full-sized riot in another game in Washington when Ben Chapman roughed up Buddy Myer, the Washington second baseman, on a slide into second. Ben and Myer rolled all over the lot, and when Ben was put out of the game—and was passing the Washington dugout—he and Whitehill got into another brawl in which we all joined.

The Washington club pulled a great play against us at the Yankee Stadium in midseason, and I guess it did as much to keep them out in front the rest of the year as anything else.

The race was very close on this day I speak of. We were trailing by a run in the ninth inning of an important game. Gehrig was on second, Dixie Walker on first, and Tony Lazzeri was at bat. There were no outs, and one of those old Yankee last-minute finishes was building up.

Tony got hold of a pitch and rammed a long line drive between Goose Goslin in right field and Sam Rice in center. Gehrig held up, halfway, expecting the ball to be caught. But Walker ducked his head and began digging around the bases.

Lou finally got under way when he saw the ball drop between Goslin and Rice and start rolling toward the fence in right center. He rounded third with Walker just a few steps behind him.

Then some remarkable things happened. At a moment when it seemed as if we were going to win the game—what with two runs about to score—Goslin made a great recovery of the ball, heaved it to Cronin, who was out on the grass in short right, and Joe turned and threw a perfect strike to Luke Sewell, the Washington catcher.

Gehrig slid into Sewell very hard. Luke tagged him out, spun around in the air, and fell on Walker—who also slid—and tagged him too, for one of the strangest plays I ever saw: a double play at home plate.

I think we went down from there.

That year, 1933, was the year of the first All-Star

game, a great stunt thought up by Arch Ward, sports editor of the Chicago *Tribune*.

It was played at Comiskey Park in Chicago, with Connie Mack in charge of the American League team and John McGraw handling the National Leaguers. I was 39 years old and not getting any livelier, but I was picked to play with the American Leaguers, including some who were young enough to be my sons.

Occasions like that have always done something to me. Maybe ballplayers like myself have a touch of the ham in them, or maybe a touch of the fire horse. But there's something about a big crowd and an event that everybody is watching or reading about or listening to. Things like that always made me want to do my best.

Anyway, I hit a home run off Wild Bill Hallahan in the third inning, with Charley Gehringer on base, and it was good enough to give the American Leaguers a 4 to 2 win. And just to show those National Leaguers—and McGraw—that I still had a few springs left in my legs, I made the top fielding play of the day—a running catch off Chick Hafey which snuffed out the National League's last rally.

But the Yanks didn't come close to the pennant that year. We were on the decline and nothing could stop it—not even the fact that Lefty Gomez won 24 that season. On August 3rd Lefty Grove shut us out, and it was the first time in 309 games that the Yanks had ever been goose-egged: a record which I doubt any team will ever touch.

At the end of the 1933 season I pulled one of the great boners of my career, but I still wonder if I could have done anything else.

When the season ended I signed up with Christy Walsh to play a series of exhibitions in the Hawaiian Islands. Christy made all plans for Claire and myself to catch a certain train to the Coast, and he had our steamship reservations from San Francisco to Honolulu all arranged. It was a very tight schedule.

We were all set to go—and would just make connections with my first engagement out there—when Frank Navin, owner of the Detroit Tigers, canned Bucky Harris as manager and made a pitch for me. He called Ed Barrow, with whom he had been associated in Detroit as a young man, and asked him if the Yanks would let me go.

"If he can improve himself," Ed said.

"I want him to manage my ball club," Navin told Ed.

"It's all right with us," Barrow answered. "But you'll have to talk to Babe."

So Navin called me and asked me to come to Detroit immediately.

I told him about the trip I had signed for; gave him the exact day on which I could get back to Detroit, and reminded him that it would be five months before his club would be in need of a manager.

He hung up, kind of distantly. Then he must have called Barrow, for Ed called me and said, "You'd better try to arrange your schedule so you can stop off in Detroit and talk to Navin."

I told him I thought I had explained things well enough to Navin. But, as it turned out, I had not.

While I was in Hawaii, Navin contacted Connie Mack and asked whether Mickey Cochrane, the A's catcher was available. Mack was hard up for cash. He sold Mickey to the Tigers for $100,000. Navin made Cochrane his manager, and when I returned to the mainland I learned I still was a private on the Yankees.

Cochrane won two pennants rights off the reel in Detroit and celebrated the second one in 1935 with the first world's championship won by a modern Detroit club. I don't know whether I could have done as well as Mickey, but I would have had pretty much the same material. In looking back over my career, I can't help but wonder whether those pennants would have gone to me instead of Mickey, if I had run out on the first part of my Hawaiian contract.

The year 1934 was my last season with the Yankees and, counting the five games I played with the Red Sox in 1914, my 21st in the American League. It wasn't a happy experience.

This time my pay had been cut to $35,000. And it was becoming more and more difficult for me to drive my legs over the outfield grass. I played in only 125 games and my batting average dropped to .288. Even so, pitchers still had enough respect for me to walk me 103 times. My home runs dropped to 22 and Gehrig finally swept by me, hitting 34.

Even though I wasn't the old Babe, I again was one of the starting outfielders when the second All-Star Game was played at the Polo Grounds in July, 1934; and I was one of that gang of five American Leaguers, Ruth, Gehrig, Foxx, Simmons and Cronin, who were struck out in that order in the second and third innings by Carl Hubbell, the great left-hander for the Giants.

Even though the National Leaguers got off to an early 4 to 0 lead on Gomez, we eventually pulled out the game by a score of 9 to 7. I'm taking nothing from Hubbell, who really put on a masterful exhibition in that game, but not enough attention is paid to Mel Harder, the American League pitcher who finished and blanked the National All-Stars with one hit for five innings. That Harder was fully as tough as old Hub. In fact he pitched 15 innings against the National Leaguers in All-Star play and they never did score a run on him.

As in 1933, the Yankees ran second in 1934, this time to Cochrane's Detroit club. They had a good lead on us on Labor Day and eventually beat us out by seven games. Schoolboy Rowe won 24 games for Mickey that year, including 16 straight.

Following the 1934 season I had a second chance to go to Japan when that same Tokyo newspaper which backed Lieb's trip in 1931 again came after me. They gave me a trunk of yen, too, for making the trip, which I was able to convert into good American dollars on our return to the States.

Though Connie Mack was the official head of our party, I ran the ball team on the field, and it was a grand trip. Unlike the 1931 trip, which was made by stars from both major leagues, this excursion was strictly an American League affair. Among the great players we had were Lou Gehrig, Jimmie Foxx, Charley Gehringer, Lefty Gomez, Earl Averill, Bing Miller, Frankie Hayes, and Earl Whitehill. Moe Berg, the man of many languages, who could talk to the Japanese in their native tongue, was our second-string catcher.

For the Gehrigs, who were married late in 1933, the trip to Japan was a belated honeymoon. The trip was a remarkable experience for all of us. Despite the treacherous attack the Japs made on us only seven years later, I cannot help but feel that the reception which millions of Japs gave us was genuine. They lined the streets of the Ginza, the Broadway of Tokyo, for miles and greeted us as though we were real heroes. Everywhere we went they feted us and tried to make our stay pleasant. No doubt there were plenty of stinkers among them; but looking back at that visit I feel it is another example of how a crackpot government can lead a friendly people into war.

We played mostly college teams and a team of Japanese All-Stars. I was surprised at their high-class fielding and the ability of some of their pitchers. But they couldn't hit a lick. We won most of our games by top-heavy scores, but that didn't discourage the crowds. They filled every stadium, and the fields at Tokyo and Kobe are bigger than anything we have outside of the Yankee Stadium and the one at Cleveland.

The Japanese set up four prizes for us to shoot at: highest batting average, home runs, runs batted in, and pitching. Some of the younger fellows might have called me "Pop" behind my back, but I won the first three prizes and Lefty Gomez won the fourth. My batting average was .408 for the whole trip.

In my living room on Riverside Drive in New York I still have the large Japanese vases on which are entered my batting exploits of that visit to Japan. But I broke up some of the other souvenirs one Sunday afternoon in December, 1941.

We played other games in Shanghai and Manila, and while most of the party returned to San Francisco, the Gehrigs, the Gomezes, Claire and I returned by way of the Suez and Mediterranean. It gave me my first chance to see Europe. I had waited a long time to see Paris but, somehow, it was a letdown. You see, a man gets accustomed to being recognized wherever he goes. One day I walked all over Paris and when I got back to the hotel Claire looked at me and said, "What's wrong, Babe?"

"Nobody gave a damn," I said.

London restored my confidence. A delegation of cricket players called on me while I was there and in the course of chewing the rag with them one of them said, "Of course, old chap, you're not accustomed to a very fast ball. No wonder you've hit well."

I asked him to repeat it, to make sure I'd heard him correctly. I guess I should have told him about Walter Johnson, Lefty Grove and a few others I had done pretty well against, but he wouldn't have understood.

Then we got around to talking about the difference in the bats used in baseball and cricket, and the same fellow said that if I could use a cricket bat in baseball I'd never have to worry about replacing it—for no one had ever broken one, as far as he remembered.

I got a sudden itch to play cricket immediately.

They took me out to Lords, or some place like that, and got the best bowler they could find to throw me a couple.

As you probably know, in cricket the bowler gives it to the batter on the first bounce, which automatically turns the pitch into what we'd call a slow ball. I hit the first pitch farther, they said, than they had ever seen a cricket ball hit.

And on the guy's second pitch I swung and broke the bat right in two.

19

Borrowed Time

The Yankees had an interesting contract waiting for me when I returned from my trip. It called for one dollar. They felt that in view of the fact that I played only 125 games in 1934, many of them contests in which I appeared in only five or six innings, and the fact that I had played baseball in the Orient well into the early winter, I would have to prove myself at the St. Petersburg training camp before they decided how much they would pay me for 1935. In the interim they wanted me under contract for a buck.

I went to Ruppert. I didn't like the idea of that provisional contract and I wanted to know my future in his organization. We again got around to the Yankee managerial question and I asked him whether he was satisfied with Joe McCarthy as a manager.

"Why, yes; aren't you?" he asked.

I told him I wasn't and felt we could have made the race closer in 1934.

Jake didn't like it, but he offered me the managership of the Newark club. I turned it down flat. Barrow then called up Claire in the hope that she could persuade me to take it. But Claire felt as I did.

"Babe, you're a big leaguer," she said. "You've been in the big leagues 21 years and you belong in the big leagues. If lesser known players rate a chance at managing, you certainly do."

Barrow's argument was that the Newark club would give me an opportunity to prove to Ruppert and himself that I had the ability to manage a ball club. He intimated that if I succeeded and showed that I had the ability to make players obey and respect me, I might some day get a crack at the Yankee job.

Remember, this was before McCarthy had won his string of pennants. Up to this point he had won only one in four years. I don't think I was talking out of turn. I just felt I had the same right to start a managerial career in the majors as Cobb, Speaker, Hornsby, Sisler, Cochrane, Harris, Cronin and others had been given.

Not so long after I had definitely turned down the Newark proposition, Judge Emil Fuchs, a former New York magistrate, who then was president of the Braves, had dinner with me at my apartment and made what looked to me like a very attractive offer. I was to have more titles than an incurable lodge joiner. I was to be vice-president of the Braves, assistant manager under Bill McKechnie, and occasionally play right field.

I didn't realize it at the time, but Fuchs, like Frazee of the old Red Sox, had bought the Braves largely on speculation and was heavily extended. He hoped that by capitalizing on my popularity and by exhibiting me in the National League he could get himself out of the red.

It was a Sunday night when the offer was made. We put through a call to Ruppert at his Garrison home on the Hudson River. After getting the Colonel I told him Fuchs wanted to speak to him. The two knew each other well for Fuchs' Braves had been our St. Petersburg training companions for years.

"I'm here in Babe Ruth's home," Fuchs yelled into the phone. "I'd like to have him on my Boston team. Is there any chance of getting him?"

I think Jake was a little upset, being called on a Sunday night. He told Fuchs he didn't do business of that kind over the phone, and suggested that the Judge and I call at his office the next morning.

At the brewery the next morning I went in first. I wanted to try once more to stay with the best organization of them all.

"Are you still satisfied with Joe McCarthy as the Yankee manager?" I asked him.

"Yes, 'Root,' I am," he answered.

Then I added, "And I suppose there is little chance that you'll change your mind."

"No chance at all," Jake said.

I turned and called in Fuchs, and what happened right after that made me a little sick.

"Colonel, I know you've had Babe on your club for many years," Fuchs boomed, "but he started in Boston and I think he should finish in Boston. I can satisfy him and keep him happy."

Ruppert suddenly handed me a paper with my unconditional release.

"I think this is what you want, isn't it, 'Root'?" he said. "After you telephoned me last night I had Barrow wire to the other American League clubs asking for waivers on you and to give us an immediate response. Every owner waives on you. I received them all this morning. You are free to sign with the Braves if that is your desire."

Fuchs had expected to pay good money to the Yankees for me.

"But what is the price; what will Babe cost me?" he asked Jake.

Ruppert looked at him.

"Do you think I would sell this man?" he asked with a strange note in his voice. "It just happens we cannot satisfy him this time, and if he can better himself elsewhere, the New York Yankees are not standing in his way."

Looking back I now realize I had the Yankees in a spot. I had slowed up, especially in the field, yet I was still so popular in New York that they didn't dare release me, nor did McCarthy dare bench me. They tried to find an answer to their problem by sending me to Newark.

I took them off the spot when I signed with the Braves.

It was pretty much of a nightmare. If I had it to do over again, the last 28 games of my 2503 and my last six home runs would never have been entered into the records.

The whole thing got off to a bad start. Bill McKechnie was not consulted before I was signed as his assistant manager. Fuchs then intimated that some day I would be the manager. It put both Bill and me in awkward positions. But we had no friction and I took my orders from him.

Some things about the new job were familiar. The Braves were still training in St. Petersburg and playing their early spring games with the Yankees. One of the pleasant events at that 1935 spring camp was that Babe Ruth, the Boston Brave, drew more at the old Waterfront Park one day than he ever had drawn as a member of the famous Yankees. Of course, I had some help. The Braves were playing the Cardinal Gas House Gang, with Dizzy and Daffy Dean, Pepper Martin, Frank Frisch, Leo Durocher and other roughnecks. We drew more than 6000 paid in a park built to seat 2500.

But I kept feeling, every time I came to bat, that this might be the last one. For the first time in my life, baseball was drudgery.

I had a lot of fun deep-sea fishing that spring. I remember once we got lost in the Gulf for about six hours. Claire telephoned the Coast Guard to search for us. Two newspapermen, Charley Segar and Marshall Hunt, my old shadow, were in the boat with me, but they were less help than I was, with that busted compass we had. Segar never was very good at direction. Once in a press box he pointed at the setting sun and asked Bill Slocum if that was west.

Old Bill looked at him and said, "If it ain't, you got yourself one hell of a story."

On another fishing trip that spring with Flint Rhem and Randy Moore, Flint hooked a big shark. He couldn't pull it in, so I blazed away at it with a .22-calibre rifle. But all I did was scare new life back into the shark. He took off with a jerk, carrying with him all of Flint's line and equipment. Flint didn't think it was funny.

During that 1935 Braves training season I was a big draw. People were curious to see how I looked in a National League uniform. But the harder I tried the worse I did. My old dogs just couldn't take it any longer. It was more and more of an effort to move over the outfield or run down to first base. I had tried hard to condition myself, but it just was torture. I was 41 and playing my 22nd season in the big leagues.

I had done some heavy hitting on that Japanese trip, but I was looking at American pitching now. The kids were striking me out or making me pop up on balls I could have hit out of the lot a few years before. It was a rotten feeling.

I recaptured a bit of the old spark on opening day in Boston. We drew a good crowd, including the governors of most of the New England states. I got a home run off Carl Hubbell and we beat the Giants. But it was just a flash, not only for me but for the Braves, who went on to lose 115 games that season.

"Stick it out for the first Western trip," Fuchs begged me, when I asked him to let me stop playing after the season opened and when I was hitting only .200.

So I went West, for the last time, and for one day in Pittsburgh I again was the old Babe Ruth. For one brief day I again wore the crown of the Sultan of Swat. For only the fourth time in my career I drove out three home runs, including the only ball that ever was driven over the right-field roof at Forbes Field.

I wish I had had sense enough to call it a career after this grand and glorious day. I wanted to, but Fuchs again talked me out of it and told me to stick for the Decoration Day games against Philadelphia. He had advertised me. I should never have listened to him.

Since he had that friendly dinner with me at my Riverside Drive apartment our relations had rapidly deteriorated. He had promised to pay me $35,000 and a percentage of profits. I quickly learned there would be no profits. In fact, Fuchs wanted me to invest $50,000 of my own money in the club. Maybe that would have been all right under the present Perini ownership, but it would have been a bad investment when Fuchs still ran the club.

He expected to cash in on me as a player. And at first, people did come out to see me, as a curiosity. But my batting average had fallen to .181 for 28 games, and people wouldn't have come out to see St. Peter himself hit .181.

My final game was the opening tilt of the holiday doubleheader against Philly on May 30, 1935. I played only a few innings and then retired for the day, with a charley horse. It was the last time my name appeared in a major league box score.

I sat on the Boston bench for the next two or three games, trying to shake off a cold, and wondering whether it would make any difference if I did.

I knew I couldn't go on another step, so on June 2, a Sunday, I asked a locker-room attendant if he'd please ask Fuchs to come down to see me for a moment.

"And you might as well tell him I'm through—for keeps," I added.

I waited a long time and at last some reporters came

in. They had strange looks on their faces. I asked them what was up.

"We're sorry, Babe," one of them said.

"Well, everything's got to end sometime," I said. "I just had to quit, that's all."

"Babe," one of them said, "you apparently haven't heard the news."

"What news?" I asked.

"You've been fired, Babe."

So I got fired before I could quit, and though Fuchs later switched it to make it appear that I had resigned, the reporters were right in the first place.

It was quite an ending.

20

It's Hard to Retire

I wanted to stay in baseball more than I ever wanted anything in my life.

But in 1935 there was no job for me, and that embittered me. I came to think that the greatest cartoon I had ever seen was one drawn at that time by Burris Jenkins, of the New York *Journal-American*, showing me walking down the road that leads away from the Yankee Stadium. Burris portrayed me in a ragged uniform, fat and elderly. A road marker, reading "To Oblivion," or something like that, pointed the way. At my heels snapped a lot of dogs, marked with such signs as "Ungrateful Owners" and "Jeering Fans," and so forth. And in the background was the Yankee Stadium, labeled, "The House that Ruth Built."

I felt completely lost at first. I thought I'd wake up and find it was a bad dream, and when it became apparent that it wasn't a dream I felt certain that the phone would ring and it would be the Yankees or some other big league team in search of me—telling me it was all a mistake. But the phone didn't ring.

I went to a lot of games at the Stadium at first, from habit I guess. But it wasn't the same, sitting in the stands and seeing somebody else in my old position and wishing I was either out there and full of pep again or connected with the Yanks in some capacity.

So after a while I began staying away from the Stadium and trying to get my mind off my disappointment. I turned to golf and played every possible hour of the day. Without it I would have blown up to 300 pounds. Without it, also, I would have gone nuts.

Instinctively, I returned to St. Pete in the late winter of 1935, as I had done for so many years before that. But, once again, sitting in the stands was a poor substitute for being a part of the Yankees. They'd call on me every once in a while, at a game, and I'd stand up in my box and wave. The people were kind and would cheer, and I'd sit down—wishing I could get out there and really give them something to cheer about.

I spent more and more time on my golf, and got good enough to hold my own in the upper flights of tournaments. In that spring of 1936, incidentally, I shot one of the best rounds of my life on the Jungle Club course at St. Pete, with Lieb, Segar and Pete Norton, a St. Pete sports writer. I remember I shot the last two holes in four under par.

It happened this way:

On the 17th, a 550-yard hole, I hit a tee shot just under 300 yards, and the ball came to rest just back of some bunkers. I reached for a wood in my bag but my little colored caddy wouldn't give it to me.

"Mr. Babe," he said, "you use a number two iron."

I told him he was daffy because there was a stiff wind blowing across the course and I had a long way to go. But he was a persistent little devil and he finally talked me into using the iron.

I poked it pretty good and got a glimpse of it as it hit near the green. But when the foursome got up to the green, my ball was nowhere in sight. We started looking in traps and the rough behind the green, and I began grousing, but suddenly the little caddy let out a yell. I turned around. He was standing right over the cup.

"Here's your ball, Mr. Babe! Here's your ball!"

It was in the cup for a double eagle—a two on a par-five hole.

On the 18th I sank a long putt for a birdie three, and thus played the last two holes in five shots instead of the regulation nine.

That was the only type of excitement in my life until midway in the 1938 season when Larry MacPhail called me up one day and asked me if I'd like to coach the Brooklyn Dodgers.

I jumped at the chance, and not only because Larry offered and paid me $15,000 for half of that season. Just to get back in a monkey suit was enough; just to get back in a ball park; to be a part of a ball club; hit the Western trips; try to outsmart the other fellow.

I was a fifth wheel and knew it, but I tried not to let it bother me. It was interesting working with the young Dodgers, telling them what I knew. And it wasn't all baseball. One day, beneath the stands at Ebbets Field, I saw a young Brooklyn player push an autograph-seeking kid roughly out of the way, and start for the dugout. For what it was worth, I said to the boy, "Here, kid, I'll sign it for you," and said it just loud enough for the player to hear me.

There were a lot of hospitals and orphanages to visit on the trips, too. I always went, and I mention it only because I think that the stars of today should take more interest in such things. I played in ten exhibition games that were suddenly added to the Dodger schedule after I joined the club. It was a daffy thing for me to do, for most of the games were played at night in small-town ballparks, and most of the kids in the box were wildly eager to strike out what was left of the home-run champ. It's a wonder I didn't get skulled.

About the time MacPhail hired me there was a story that he had been talked into it by Leo Durocher, then captain of the Dodgers—who were managed by Burleigh Grimes. The truth was, of course, that Larry hired me on his own. He is a showman and a natural promoter, and he thought I could become the first coach ever to draw any customers. Maybe I was, at that. Our exhibitions grossed $14,000.

As for Leo and myself, we didn't get along nearly as well as we had when I was the big shot on the Yanks. One day he loudly accused me of missing a signal, and I just as loudly told him he was nuts. We had trouble speaking after that and when it was announced after the 1938 season that Leo had been named manager, I knew I wouldn't return to the Dodgers.

Even while I was in Dodger uniform, the Yankees remained my first love. Joe McCarthy had whipped together another great Yankee team, built around the remains of some of the older Yanks—such as Lou Gehrig—but sparked by Joe DiMaggio, Joe Gordon, Tommy Henrich, Charley Keller and younger fellows like that.

I rooted for Lou to hold his own in this new combination, and to keep putting his consecutive games record out of any future player's reach. And for a long, long time he came through. But then I began to hear some strange stories about the Dutchman. One, particularly, made me certain that something had gone haywire with him. A wild left-hander on the Washington team, Joe Krakauskas, gave out an interview one day that he was afraid to throw his fast one to Lou because Lou had a habit of leaning into an inside pitch instead of backing away. Krakauskas even said he was certain that he had thrown a ball inside Gehrig's wrists—or between the loop formed by Lou's arms as he "took it."

Lou had a terrible spring season in 1939, and then sent word to me that he was going to the Mayo Clinic for a checkup. In June of 1939 the country learned the worst, that he had a rare form of infantile paralysis. His great streak ended at 2130 games.

He went down and down, physically, but it just didn't seem possible to me. From the time I first saw him—when we mistook him for Zbysko—he had always seemed the last word in muscular strength to me. He could have broken an oak tree in two with his hands. Now here he was, dragging himself along, losing his balance and clutching at the air—and, in the end, becoming too weak to light a match.

No matter how long I live, I'll never forget the least detail of the Gehrig Day at the Stadium—July 4, 1939. Barrow brought a lot of the old Yanks back to say farewell to Lou, and we lined up along one side of the plate: Meusel, Pennock, Hoyt, Pipp, Lazzeri, Schang, Koenig, Dugan, Bengough, Pipgras and some others. The new Yanks were on the other side, and after a while Lou came up from the dugout and stood at home plate.

I couldn't look at him when he began to talk, after Jim Farley, Mayor LaGuardia, Jimmy Walker, McCarthy, Dan Daniel and the others had had their say.

Lou spoke as I never thought I'd hear a man speak in a ball park. Every word he said plainly came from his heart, and the big crowd of more than 60,000 sat there in the stands and there wasn't a dry eye anywhere. The Dutchman spoke of Mom and Pop Gehrig, and Eleanor, his wife, and what the Yanks had meant to him, and when he said, "I consider myself the luckiest man in the world," I couldn't stand it any longer.

I went over to him and put my arm around him, and though I tried to smile and cheer him up, I could not keep from crying.

Something like this could never happen again, I told myself. And yet I was destined to stand at the same home plate—only seven years later—in much the same condition and under much the same circumstances.

I became a kind of ornament or antique of baseball history. That same year my old sparring mate, Judge Landis, invited me up to the Hall of Fame at Cooperstown for the opening of the museum. It was good to see the tough old guy again, and the old ball-players who were able to be there: Cobb, Hans Wagner, Speaker, Nap Lajoie, Eddie Collins, Walter Johnson, Grover Cleveland Alexander, Cy Young, George Sisler and Connie Mack.

The war came along and, indirectly, it brought about my last appearance in uniform in the Yankee Stadium. In the summer of 1942, Walter Johnson and I put on an exhibition for the benefit of the Army-Navy Relief. I hadn't had a bat in my hand for four years, and Walter hadn't thrown a ball in that time.

It made quite a show and brought back a lot of memories. I had pitched against Walter in my days with the Red Sox, and batted against him for many years after that. No one could ever throw a ball as hard as Walter. Yet everybody who ever hit against him took a toe hold on the plate. They knew that Walter wouldn't throw at them and that he wouldn't doctor up the ball so that it might "take off," and skull them. Walter always believed in trying to get along without any sharpshooting. If he had gone in for any trickery, he would have left behind him a pitching record which nobody ever would have touched. What he did leave behind was greater—a remarkable pitching record and a wonderful name.

"Babe, I just want to ask one thing," he said to me in his kind way as we waited under the stands for our cue to go out on the field. "Don't hit any back at me."

I told him I'd be lucky to hit any at all, but that if I did get hold of one I'd make sure I pulled it.

We went out on the field and it was one of the great thrills of my life in the game. The crowd that day numbered 60,000 and there was a new and lustier note in it—because of the war. It stood on its hind legs and gave us a terrific ovation.

Johnson took his place and threw a couple to Benny Bengough behind the plate. The catcher had to jump for the first one, but then Walter found the groove. I stepped into his third pitch and knocked it in the lower right-field stands.

Walter threw me 21 pitches. On the 21st all the cobwebs seemed to drop off my baseball muscles. I gave it everything I had and hit it up into third deck in right field, one of the comparatively few balls ever hit up there. That was enough for me. I knew I couldn't top that, so I trotted around the bases and the little show was over.

They were still yelling for us as we disappeared into the Yankee dugout and started down to the dressing room. We walked along, gabbing and signing autographs, but there was a kind of sadness in both of us. Walter had been the greatest pitcher in the league; I had been the greatest slugger. But he was no longer a part of the game, and the same was true of me.

Cobb and I got the same feeling that year when we played a few Red Cross golf exhibitions. It's hard to be on the outside of something you love. Just looking in doesn't help.

It probably would have been easier if it hadn't been for the fans. From the mail I got—and always answered—and the receptions I had every place I went, and every place I drove or walked or flew, I felt that the public was as bewildered over my absence from baseball as I was. A second-stringer can go back to the farm or get some other kind of job and fit into the routine of life. But I had had too much publicity, had been too well-known, had been too much a part of baseball for that to happen. And if the public was ever inclined to forget me, some sports columnist would come along and write a piece wondering why baseball had "forsaken the biggest drawing card it ever had."

As was inevitable, baseball went down and down during the second World War, and the fans—including myself—began to hearken back to the baseball of prewar vintage, to the baseball of the late 1930's, and the late 1920's and the years before that.

Occasionally I'd get a request from a magazine or newspaper to pick my All-Star Team, but I'd never get around to sending it in. I thought about the past a lot, however, and in my mind I did pick a team, a team that would have beaten any combination that ever lived, and that includes the greatest club ever assembled for regular competition—the 1927 Yankees.

I give my All-Star Team here for the first time:

PITCHERS: Walter Johnson
                 Christy Mathewson
                 Grover Cleveland Alexander
                 Herb Pennock
CATCHER: Ray Schalk
FIRST BASE: Hal Chase
SECOND BASE: Nap Lajoie
THIRD BASE: Jimmy Collins
SHORTSTOP: Hans Wagner
OUTFIELDERS: Ty Cobb
                 Tris Speaker
                 X

Except for Jimmy Collins, I saw or played with or against every man on that mythical club. A lot of fans, especially in New York, will be surprised that I haven't picked more Yankees or Giants and have not picked a Dodger.

They, and others, will feel that I should pick Lou Gehrig over Chase. Or George Sisler over both of them. But I pick Chase. I saw him first in spring training before the start of the first World War. I felt the sting of his tremendous ability in that angry Red Sox-Giants exhibition tour in 1919. Hal had been in the big show for 15 years then, but he was so much better than anybody I ever saw on first base that—to me—it was no contest, and I still feel that way.

We've got some nice first basemen in the game today, and maybe once a year you'll see one of them charge a would-be sacrifice—with a man on second, heading for third—and throw out the runner at third. Hal would do it dozens of times a year. He even did it on the third-base side of the pitcher.

I believe he was just about the quickest thinker I ever saw in baseball. He was always one thought ahead of the runner. His trouble—if he had one—was he was too smart. He had to wait for the reflexes of his fellow infielders to function, which were often too slow.

Chase left baseball under a cloud. Maybe if he had been tossed out when Landis was in charge of the game he would have been as looked down on today as the worst of the Black Sox. I don't know. All I know is that he was—for my dough—the greatest first baseman who ever lived. That he was thrown out of the game is a tragedy, but that doesn't lower his ability in my eyes, any more than the banishment of Shoeless Joe Jackson will ever make me doubt that he was the most natural and graceful hitter who ever lived.

Chase couldn't hit as far as Gehrig or as consistently as Sisler. But he was no punk at the plate. He was good enough to lead the National League in hitting while playing with Cincinnati. And he was one of the best base runners the game ever produced. I pick him primarily for his unbelievable fielding ability, however, and I still say that in any tight game—where tight fielding has as much importance as hitting—I'd rather have him on my team than any other first baseman in the game's history.

I put Larry Lajoie on second with the full knowledge that I am passing over such other great second basemen as Eddie Collins, Rogers Hornsby, Charley Gehringer and Frankie Frisch. But in my book Larry is the best.

When I was a green rookie, less than a half year

out of St. Mary's, the first big league team I faced in scheduled competition was Cleveland. Larry then was in his 19th year of big league ball, but he still retained his easygoing grace and remarkable hitting skill. Lajoie could make the hardest chances look easy. There never was any frantic racing around for a ball hit near him; Larry just seemed to glide over the ground and get in perfect position for the fielding play.

In my experience I never knew a better batsman for protecting the runner on the hit-and-run play. No matter where the ball was pitched, Larry would hit it. He would reach out for it or throw his bat at it if necessary. The pitcher just couldn't get the ball past him.

Larry was the American League's batting champion before Cobb came on the scene. He once hit over .400, and I'm wondering what he could do to that double jack rabbit ball used in the big leagues today.

At shortstop there is only one candidate, the immortal Honus Wagner. He was just head and shoulders over anyone else in that position. Fellows like Marion, Bancroft, Peck, and Billy Jurgess were all great fielders. But Honus could more than out-field all of them. He was perhaps the greatest right-handed hitter of all time. He had remarkably long arms, big hams for hands, and just drew the ball to him. Ed Barrow once told me he could have been as good in any position but he made his greatest name as shortstop. He led the National League seven times at bat and he always was up with the leaders when he was in his forties.

As I said, Jimmy Collins is the only one on my All-Star Team I did not actually see. However, while playing in Boston during my first six years I heard plenty about him, for he starred on both the Boston Nationals and the Red Sox.

So many old-timers told me what a wonder he was that he must have been one of baseball's immortal players. He could come in and pounce on bunts or short hits like a cat, but if anyone tried to cross him up and rifle a hard drive through him, Jimmy always was ready. Nothing got by him.

He was the hardest hitting third baseman of his day. From what they tell me, he could do everything— bunt, place hits or push them past the outfielders. Connie Mack placed him on third base on his team. That's enough of an endorsement for any ballplayer.

No one can dispute Ty's right to be placed on anyone's All-Star Team. I had numerous arguments and run-ins with Cobb. At times we wanted to cut each other to ribbons. But neither of us ever carried those arguments out of the clubhouse. I have a sincere and honest respect for Ty Cobb and his great ability. He had the highest lifetime average of anyone who ever played big league baseball (.367), was a whippet on the bases (he stole 892 of them), and was a player with an unbeatable competitive spirit. Not too many players liked Cobb when he played ball. Ty always went all out to win. On the base lines he demanded the right of way. If an infielder tried to block him or get in his way, it was just too bad.

My old Red Sox side-kick, Tris Speaker, wins center field in my book, even though I recognize that Joe DiMaggio of the present-day Yankees is a greater center fielder. But "Spoke" was something extra-special. Only those who played with or against him really appreciated what a great ballplayer he was.

I know that back in my Red Sox pitching days I would hear the crack of an enemy's bat and say, "There goes the ball game." But Tris would turn his back to the plate, race far out to the fences and at the last moment make a diving catch. Not once, like Al Gionfriddo pulling down DiMaggio's drive in the 1947 World Series, but a thousand times.

He was more than a great outfielder; he actually was a fifth infielder. Tris would play close and get many balls in short center or right field and occasionally throw a runner out at first. Maybe with the present lively ball Tris couldn't play that way. But he could still go out for them, and with the modern ball his great hitting would be much greater.

Tris was a great base runner, not quite up to Cobb but ahead of most of the others. It just happened that when Speaker was in his prime so was Cobb, and Ty was such a competitor in both hitting and running that he would let no one finish ahead of him. In fact when Cobb won 11 batting championships in 12 years, the only one who broke through on him was Tris Speaker.

I place a big "X" in right field. Maybe that's false modesty, but I just don't want to pick myself. Claire says, "Don't be silly, Babe, there couldn't be any All-Star Team without you." Maybe she is right; but just the same, I prefer to put "X" in that spot and let the reader pick out that position.

I'll even recommend some great right fielders, among them: Harry Hooper of the old Red Sox club, Joe Jackson, the fellow I patterned my swing after, Harry Heilmann, the hard-hitting Detroit outfielder, and Ross Youngs, McGraw's old right fielder who used to drive the Yankees daffy when we played the Giants in those early World Series of 1921, 1922 and 1923. And Youngs' great successor, Mel Ott, whose 511 National League home runs should stand for many years to come.

For catcher my man is Ray Schalk, the durable little iron man who caught for the White Sox for so many years and had the catching record for games caught until Al Lopez beat him during the war years. Schalk wasn't as good a hitter as Bill Dickey, Gabby Hartnett or Roger Bresnahan, but to me he was the perfect catcher.

In the many years that I played against him I was always impressed with his smartness behind the plate. Even when the White Sox had terrible teams after the sellout scandal they usually made good showings against the far stronger Yankees. It was largely due to Schalk's careful coaching of his pitchers and his letting them know just how to pitch to us and what were our weaknesses.

He was one of the greatest throwers I've ever seen, pegging down to the bases like a shot. I think if you look back at his record you'll find he had very few wild throws or passed balls. No matter where some of those wild Chicago pitchers would throw, little Ray would have his glove up there and knock down the ball if he couldn't actually catch it. He wasn't a .300 hitter, but always bothered you when he came up in the clutch.

You can take my four pitchers, Johnson, Mathewson, Alexander and Pennock in any order.

I don't need to tell the present generation of fans how good Walter Johnson was. They tell me that in his very early years in the league he was a thrower who depended on his speed to blow the ball past the batsman. Of course, that's the same accusation they brought against me when I was a 23-game winner with the Red Sox.

I know by the time I came into the league Johnson not only had terrific speed but he always knew what to pitch. Rarely did he ever make a mistake on the mound. Naturally, as he grew older, he acquired additional polish. Walter was voted the American League's most valuable player in 1925, in his 19th year in the league, a remarkable achievement for an athlete.

You need a certain number of breaks in baseball and every other calling. Johnson got a minimum of them. He spent his entire pitching life with Washington, usually in the second division and sometimes in last place. It was not until he was 37 that he got into a World Series. If he had been fortunate enough to pitch for such clubs as the old Red Sox or the latter-day Yankees there is no telling what records he would have hung up. He lost a heartbreaking number of 1 to 0 and 2 to 1 games.

My career and that of the great Christy Mathewson overlapped for only about three seasons. I came in with the Red Sox in 1914 and Matty went out with the Reds two years later. I saw him pitch only a few games, but I know he belongs among the pitching immortals.

They used to say his catchers, Bresnahan and later Chief Meyers, could catch him sitting in a rocking chair. And it was said that if a dime were placed on the plate Matty could pitch a ball right over it. His control was so great that he once pitched 68 consecutive innings without allowing a walk. He won three shutouts in the 1905 World Series.

Matty died of tuberculosis while still a comparatively young man. But as a ballplayer he had a great physique and was a tremendous work horse. He won 37 games in 1908 though the Giants failed to win the pennant.

As for old Aleck, I played against him in World Series that were years apart, the 1915 Red Sox-Philly Series and the 1926 and 1928 Series between the Yankees and Cardinals. I saw "Ol' Pete" when he was in his very prime and when, in 1926, he snatched a World Series right out of our laps. What made it more remarkable was that he wasn't a fellow who took the best care of himself. But he had a great head on his shoulders and the courage of a lion. Alexander was just a born pitcher.

Naturally, one left-hander belongs on my staff, and I pick my old teammate of Boston and New York days, Herb Pennock. He was a left-handed Mathewson. Though weighing little more than 165 pounds, he had one of the easiest, most graceful deliveries of any pitcher I have ever known. Certainly Rube Waddell and Lefty Grove had more smoke, but they didn't have Pennock's class. He was a real artist on the mound, doing with his artistry what Waddell and Grove did with their superior speed.

In selecting a four-man pitching staff to go with my All-Stars I realize I have had to pass up many of the great pitching names of baseball; many men for whom I have had the greatest respect: old Cy Young, Eddie Plank, Chief Bender, Jack Coombs, Mordecai Brown, and the present Bobby Feller. Bobby is now at a stage in his career when he still is effective, but not as much so as when his great speed was sufficient for him to throw the balls past the hitters. A pitcher's greatness is measured by his ability to adapt himself when he loses his youthful speed and really must start pitching.

Anyway, that's my team. Maybe we'll all get together someday in a happier world. If we do—don't bet against us.

Before I leave the war years, I want to tell a story which I don't believe is very well known.

In the fading months of the war I was nearly called upon to act as a peace negotiator. My friend of long standing, Paul Carey, who served in the Navy during the war, was the author of the plan that would have sent me to the Pacific.

This country made frequent broadcasts to the Japanese people during the war, but without any great effect. After the Germans folded, we looked around for new methods of getting the Japs to quit committing suicide and surrender.

Carey thought of me because of the surprising popularity I had enjoyed during my trip to Japan in the middle 1930's. He submitted a plan whereby I was to be flown to Guam and there placed aboard a destroyer which was to be painted white.

The destroyer would have carried me to a point off the coast of Japan and I was to have made a series of broadcasts to the Japanese people. I was to appeal to their sporting instincts; tell them what we had in store for them if they didn't give up, and assure them that surrender was a lot better than annihilation.

The plan, of course, fell through. It just wasn't in keeping with the great overall plans of the Army, Navy and Air Force. They had reached the ninth inning and they had their best sluggers coming up. But I wish I could have helped, someway.

21

The End—It Seemed

In September, 1946, a number of persons very close to me, including Claire, Paul Carey, Charles Schwepel, and my attorney, Melvyn Gordon Lowenstein, and a number of others began commenting that my voice was getting hoarser.

I had noticed it myself, but believed it was just some sort of reaction to the old scalding it got from that "treatment" when I was a rookie. Or, when I didn't think it was that, I believed it had something to do with my sinus trouble.

I began to get very severe pains over my left eye, but I'd take a couple of aspirins and try to forget them. More important than any pain over the eye was another pain.

The Yankees had turned me down again. Early in 1946 I decided that I might have been wrong in demanding a chance to start out as a big league manager—though a lot of fellows who had had considerably less experience than I got the chance.

So when Bill Dickey signed his 1946 contract as a player, thus ending the talk that he'd go to Newark as manager, I called up Larry MacPhail—then running the Yankee organization—and asked him for the Newark job.

My phone call, he told me, was "a thunderbolt out of the sky," but he seemed pleased and said he'd call me back in a few days. After two weeks had passed, without a call from him, I called again. This time he said that George Weiss (who was destined to succeed him, but who at that time was head of the Yankee farm system) was in Chicago and that the club would get in touch with me as soon as Weiss returned.

After another two weeks of waiting, I called Mac-Phail again. I had a little trouble getting him, but when I did he told me that they were planning to hire somebody else. I guess I have no complaint coming there. Larry represented a completely new deal in the Yankee front office. He didn't owe me a thing.

About this time, the Mexican League was making raids on the major leagues that reminded me of the old days of the Federal League. Jorge Pasquel, the main power behind Mexican baseball, contacted me and invited me down to look over his operation. He made me a very attractive offer; in fact an offer many times better than I had ever gotten in either the American or National Leagues.

But I turned it down. I still believed that a job would open up for me in my own country.

No job appeared. So I went on playing golf, waiting and hoping. The summer of 1946 drifted by, and, as I said, in the fall of that year my friends began to notice what had long been noticeable to me—my failing physical condition.

By November of 1946 the pain over my eye was so intense, night and day, that Dr. Philip MacDonald, who had been treating my throat and sinus, suggested that I enter French Hospital in New York for observation. I went in a wheel chair.

At first it was believed that my trouble must be coming from three bad teeth. I had them extracted, but the pain continued. Then Dr. MacDonald, after consulting Claire, Carey and Lowenstein, began calling in specialists: Dr. H. M. Wertheim, a neurosurgeon; Dr. Byron Stookey, head of the neurological institute at the Medical Center; Dr. J. Lawrence Pool; Dr. Robert H. McConnell and several others.

For days the X-rays showed nothing, but my condition got worse. Then, one of the plates did show something, and they decided to cut me.

I knew nothing of the decision at the time it was made. But even if I had, it would have made little difference to me, so great was the pain in my head. As a matter of fact, my head became paralyzed about that time. My left eye dropped shut and I lost my ability to swallow. I seldom could speak.

On the night before I was cut, Paul Carey, my friend for 18 years and a good Catholic, sat for some time at my bedside without speaking. But when he did speak he got right to the point.

"You're going to be okay, Babe," Paul said. "Nothing's ever going to get you down. But they're going to operate tomorrow morning. Don't you think you ought to get your house in order?"

I knew what he meant. I had drifted away from the Church during my harum-scarum early years in the majors. I'd go to Mass now and then and, believe me, I never missed a night without saying my prayers. But I wasn't the Catholic I had been at St. Mary's, especially after Brother Matthias died about the time my baseball career was ending.

I could speak a little now, and I told Paul that he was right; that I did want my house in order.

He had a chaplain standing by. I made my Confession, and when it was done he told me he'd come back in the morning and give me Holy Communion.

"Don't bother about fasting, Babe," he said to me. "It'll be all right."

"I'll fast," I said, and I did.

Holy Communion gave me additional heart to face a very delicate operation that kept me on the table for a long time. They dug into my neck and tied up or dug out the nerves that were transmitting pain from the seat of my trouble to my eye and jaws and head in general.

When they could move me they wheeled me back in front of the X-ray machines again and gave me so many treatments that the roots of my hair on one side of my head were rotted. My hair came out in hunks when the nurses tried to comb it.

I was fed for weeks with a needle, for I had no strength to swallow. I don't recommend that kind of eating. No taste. I lost 80 pounds, and there were times when I felt I would die. It is a rotten feeling for a man who was as active as I was.

Then I began to sense that the stands were rooting for me—the sincerest rooting I had ever had. Claire was there with me, night and day, and Gordon Lowenstein and Paul and the few others who were permitted to see me.

And outside the walls of the hospital, and across the greatest city in the world, and out across the country and the world, the fans who had known me as a ballplayer were rooting.

I couldn't believe it, at first. Lying in that little room I often felt so alone that the tears would run helplessly down my cheeks. But then Claire began bringing in some letters, and Gordon brought in pocketfuls of them and Paul brought in boxes of them. And they read them to me.

No man ever got letters like those. Before I left the hospital there were 30,000 of them. Most of them were written in the penciled scrawl of kids, and telling me that I was going to get well. Most of these boys had never seen me play; in fact some of them had not been born when I stopped playing. But they seemed to look upon me as a friend in need of comfort—and I was.

I could read some of them after a while. The one from Mike Quinlan of Jersey City, for instance.

"Dear Babe," he wrote. "Everybody in the seventh grade class is pulling and praying for you. I am enclosing a medal and holy picture which if you wear will make you better.

"You're Pal—Mike Quinlan.

"P.S.—I know this will be you're 61 homer. You will hit it."

I pinned the *Miraculous Medal* on my pajama coat, and it is still there.

And the one from Brother Gilbert, who had helped me get my first break in baseball. Brother Gilbert, who was to die so soon after that, led his class of boys in prayers for my recovery.

There were letters from public officials and from GI's here and abroad; from veterans' hospitals and sports figures, including my old friend Jack Dempsey who wired, "Keep your chin up. And keep punching, which I know you will." Toots Shor called me daily to ask what I wanted to eat, and sent it up from his restaurant.

But it was the letters from the kids that really touched me, and I made up my mind, once again, that I'd find some way to get better and help them, especially the ones who were in as much need of help as I once had been.

I insisted that every letter be answered. The actual job of writing replies was attended to by Carey, Lowenstein and my good friend May Singhi Breen, the radio star. But I signed them. In fact that's the one thing I'll never give to any person—the right to sign my name for me.

My last days in the hospital were busy ones. On February 3, 1947, I had my first visitors—Baseball Commissioner Happy Chandler and Frank Stevens. I hated for them to see me the way I looked, and could not keep from crying when they did. I was that weak. They cried, too, after telling me I'd be okay.

On February 7th, my 52nd birthday, the doctors let me make some kind of reply to the thousands of letters and messages that had come into the hospital. I sent out this word:

"I'm fighting hard and I'll soon be on top. I thank everyone from the bottom of my heart for their messages and good wishes."

Peter De Rose, the composer, and husband of May Singhi Breen, brought in a birthday cake. And a wire from Connie Mack.

"Hope you have many more happy birthdays and pass my 84 years," Connie wired. "You deserve all the good things the sportswriters are saying about you. May God bless you for all you have done for the youth of America."

It *was* a happy birthday.

I left the hospital on February 15, 1947, and, from the looks of me, I guess a lot of people thought that I was being sent home to die. But I had much to live for, and though I was in great pain, it was comforting to get back with Claire to the apartment where I had spent the happiest years of my life.

A lot of people wanted to see me, but Claire and the others guarded me carefully. One of the first outsiders I saw was Stan Lomax, the sports broadcaster who had always been a good pal of mine. The first and only ballplayer I saw during these early days of my convalescence was Hank Greenberg, who came up to see me one snowy morning at a time when he couldn't decide whether to stay in baseball or quit.

I urged him to take the job Pittsburgh had offered him.

"A man's got to keep playing, if he's fit," I said. "But keep looking out for yourself. Keep your wind. That's everything.

"You'll like the National League, Hank," I told him. "Especially the ball parks. I got a bum break when I went over there, but that was just accidental. You'll be okay. They'll curve-ball you a lot, and you'll find they think a one-run lead is something nice to sit back and rest on. But otherwise it's the same baseball we played.

"Don't quit until every base is uphill."

On March 8, 1947, Commissioner Chandler announced that Sunday, April 27th, would be "Babe Ruth Day" in every ball park in organized baseball.

Chandler's statement read:

"All Americans and others interested in sports throughout the world have been concerned in recent months over the illness of one of baseball's most beloved figures.

"George Herman (Babe) Ruth is now recuperating from a serious operation.

"In order that fans, players and the management of the game might have an opportunity to unite in a salute and join in a prayer for his early recovery, Sunday, April 27, has been designated 'Babe Ruth Day.' Appropriate ceremonies will be held at every major league game. A nation-wide system will carry a special broadcast.

"The commissioner earnestly hopes that every lover of baseball will participate.

"There will be no collection—no advance in prices at the parks. This is not a fund raising event. It is an expression of affection to one who has contributed so much to our national sport—baseball."

There were so many suggestions, immediately, that I should get a portion of the receipts of the ball games that I had to make a public statement that I didn't want a quarter for myself, but that if any money was presented to me it should be turned over to the kids who needed it.

I guess that was the birth, in my mind, of the Babe Ruth Foundation, Inc., which was later set up to provide funds for the mental and physical education of underprivileged American boys.

On April 7, 1947, a corporation came forward with the idea that I should maintain a contact with the game of baseball. The Ford Motor Company, under-writing the American Legion Junior Baseball League, retained me to travel around that circuit—with nurses and a near-by physician—to appear before the boys, offer them what advice I had to give on baseball and sportsmanship and life in general, and help with league matters.

It was, and remains, the kind of job I'd always hoped I'd have, though I wish I had the strength, and authority, to expand it to adult fans. Still, the Ford Company's act is to my mind the finest kind of public service and I'm proud to be a part of it.

I went on a fishing trip after signing up with Benson Ford. Ray Kilthau, an old friend, had me down to his place in Miami. Ray protected me from a lot of people—I couldn't talk to them because my voice sounded like somebody gargling ashes—and I had plenty of time to fish. I was pretty weak, but I managed to land a 50-pound sailfish and even played a little golf.

That first golf of mine, after my illness, was a strange experience. I retained my old manner of ad-dressing the ball, and my old swing. I gave each drive everything I had, but what I had was pathetic. I used to hit balls occasionally 300 yards off the tee. Now with the same motion, and the same intent, I was hitting them 150 yards. It was a bum feeling.

I came back for "Babe Ruth Day" in New York, and had a pleasant surprise the day before. The New York *News* dug up Johnny Sylvester and brought him over to my apartment. I had not seen him for years, of course; in fact I hadn't seen him since the day when I called on him as he lay on his sickbed in 1926.

In the meantime, he had gone to Princeton, become a Navy Lieutenant in the South Pacific, and was now head of a Long Island machine-making firm.

"Gosh, I hope he remembers me this time," Johnny said to Claire before I came into the living room where he was waiting.

"He'll remember you; don't worry," Claire said.

I walked in and held out my hand. "Hello, Johnny," I said, "I haven't seen you since you were a skinny little kid."

"Hello, Babe," he said. "I'm grown up now, thanks to you. And I figured it was only right for me to visit you, after your visit to me—a long time ago—did me so much good."

"Babe Ruth Day" was the most impressive thing that ever happened to me. There were nearly 60,000 in the Yankee Stadium when I walked out to home plate, and my thoughts reeled back to the day when poor old Lou Gehrig made the same hard trip from the dugout.

The speeches were just about the same as when Lou had been honored, with one great exception. Francis Cardinal Spellman, who was a pretty good ballplayer himself as a young man, and who has never lost his interest in the game, was part of the program. He composed and spoke a great prayer for baseball, and for me. This was it:

"O God of life and love and health, creator of all men, we beg Thee to descend upon us with Thy light, Thy strength, and Thy peace; to bless our nation and all nations; to bless each person in every land.

"To Thee, we turn today and pray Thee: Be the spirit of our sports, the source of our spiritual inspiration and physical strength, for the upbuilding of our nation as, on this occasion, we honor a hero in the world of sport, a champion of fair play and a manly leader of youth in America.

"We beseech Thee to bless him and his apostolate among the youth of every land that he may continue to encourage and inspire the young to live chaste, sober and heroic lives, that they may build for themselves bodies disciplined by the highest ideals of sportsmanship for the glory of our beloved country, for the glory of Thy beloved Self.

"Thou has made the hearts of children and youth to rejoice and to benefit from the gladness they find in their games. Thou has given them a divinely created instinct for play, laughter and joy. And today we beg Thy peace for the sake of these same youthful hearts that they may learn to know, to love and to live Thy goodness not only in their sports and games, but also in the love of man, race for race and nation for nation.

"O, life-giving Father in Heaven, whose breath is life to man's body, whose spirit is health to man's soul, bless Thou with especial love him whom we honor here this day; grant upon him, O God, Thy tender mercies for ever more. Amen."

Mel Allen, a great baseball announcer, introduced me. I didn't have much voice left by then, for I had had a very bad coughing spell just before going on the field. But I tried to get across a point as best I could.

"You know this baseball game of ours comes up from the youth," I said, hardly recognizing my voice as it came back to me from the loud-speakers. "That means the boys. And after you're a boy and grow up to play ball, then you come to the boys you see representing clubs today in your national pastime."

I gestured toward the new Yankees, lined up near the plate.

"The only real game, I think, in the world is baseball. As a rule people think that if you give boys a football or a baseball or something like that they naturally become athletes right away.

"But you can't do that in baseball. You've got to start from away down at the bottom, when the boys are six or seven years of age. You can't wait until they're 15 or 16. You've got to let it grow up with you, if you're the boy. And if you try hard enough you're bound to come out on top, just as these boys here have come to the top now.

"There have been so many lovely things said about

me today," I finished, "that I'm glad to have had the opportunity to thank everybody. Thank you."

I walked back toward the dugout, and the way they yelled for me made tears come again to my eyes.

Cardinal Spellman was in the dugout. He caught me by the arm.

"Babe," he said, "you've been an inspiration to all creeds. You've always been an inspiration to me. Good luck and God bless you."

I didn't know what to say, hearing a man as great as Cardinal Spellman telling me I had been an inspiration to him.

Then he said, "Babe, I heard about what happened at the hospital. If you want me to, I'll come up to your apartment and give you Communion some Sunday."

It was too much. I shook my head.

"I'll come down to your place," I said.

Gordon Lowenstein drew up the papers for the Babe Ruth Foundation, Inc., early in May and we announced it on May 8, 1947. As directors we were able to get Commissioner Chandler; Ford Frick, President of the National League; Will Harridge, President of the American League; Grantland Rice, the dean of American sports writers and a close personal friend; my good friends, Paul Carey, and Emory C. Perry, Chicago industrialist; Mr. Lowenstein and, later, Eric Johnston, head of the Motion Picture Producers and Distributors group.

The purpose of the Foundation is "to receive and maintain a fund or funds and to apply the income thereof, together with so much of the principal thereof as may be deemed necessary, to supporting, aiding and assisting financially or otherwise, charitable, educational, religious, scientific, literary, artistic, benevolent, philanthropic, humanitarian and eleemosynary uses, causes, undertakings, enterprises and projects of every kind, nature and description whatsoever."

Lowenstein explained it further.

"In effect," he told the reporters who came to his office for particulars, "the funds will be used to aid American youngsters to achieve good character from participation in sports and to offer scholarships and prizes to underprivileged boys, not necessarily connected with sports."

Aside from my own, the first contribution made to the foundation came on the last day of the 1947 baseball season when Larry MacPhail, who was soon to quit the Yankees, brought together a great collection of old-time stars and coaxed them into playing two innings of baseball. It was a wonderful gesture on Larry's part, and I'll always be grateful.

In addition, he easily persuaded Connie Mack, whose Athletics were playing the Yanks in the regular game that day, to turn over his share of the day's receipts—there were 25,000 in the stands—to the Foundation.

What a game those old fellows put on; what a great feeling it was to be with them again!

Cobb was there (Del Webb, one of the Yankee owners, had picked him up in Las Vegas, Nev., and flown him East in a private plane), and Speaker, Cy Young, Hooper, Lewis, Al Simmons, Sisler, Joe Judge, Jimmy Foxx, Home Run Baker, Wally Schang, Mickey Cochrane, Lefty Grove, Wally Pipp, Herb Pennock, Bob Meusel, Earle Combs, Red Rolfe, George Selkirk, Waite Hoyt, Lefty Gomez, Red Ruffing, Chief Bender, Roger Peckinpaugh, Buddy Hassett, Johnny Sturm, Billy Evans, Tommy Connolly, Big Ed Walsh and so many others that they made my head swim.

I had hoped to be able to get back in my old Yankee uniform and pitch to the first batter, but I just didn't feel up to it. I was a spectator that day, and never enjoyed watching a game more than that one.

Cobb was the first of the old-time All-Stars to step to the plate. Hoyt was in the box for the old Yankees.

And right then and there, Ty showed a younger generation of fans why we called him the cagiest player who ever lived.

He turned around to Wally Schang (behind the plate), and said, "Wally, I haven't had a bat in my hands for years. I'm afraid it might slip out of my hands when I swing. Would you please step back a yard or so?"

Wally did, and Ty laid down a bunt in front of the plate on the next pitch!

In the second inning, Tris hit a double to left and ran it out like a schoolboy, a sight to remember. But in the last half of the second—and last—inning, the old Yanks came on as they had so many times in their earlier days in the game. With two men on base (Lefty Gomez, the worst hitter since Wilcy Moore, actually was one of them), Combs hit one over Speaker's head in center for an inside-the-park home run to win the game.

That's why I'll always be a Yankee.

In June, 1947, the pains came back to me and they were almost as severe as they had been just before and just after my operation. Though I tried not to show it, and tried to "shake it off," it was impossible. I couldn't sleep. My jaws were so sensitive that sometimes I'd double over in pain while eating, even if I bit down on something as soft as the white of a two-minute egg.

Dr. MacDonald worried about this and gathered the old board of strategy once again. I didn't know about it, for they did not want to worry me.

Then one day he came to me and said he was going to give me a shot. I asked no questions, but I could see from his manner that it was something special.

I soon found out that this type of treatment had rarely been used on a human being before. There was a chance that it would prove nothing, and there was also the chance that it might prove harmful to me in my condition. I was in very bad shape.

The matter was left up to me. It wasn't an easy decision. I had been so close to being called out—for keeps—that just being able to get around a bit each day was a kind of reprieve that might have satisfied me. But then I realized that if anything was learned about that type of treatment, whether good or bad, it would be of use in the future to the medical profession and maybe to a lot of people with my same trouble.

So I took the shots.

They've put weight back on what had become pretty much of a rattling skeleton. I lost about 70 pounds during the worst part of my illness. In fact, when I was at last able to stand up and look myself over I was surprised to see my feet down below me. It was the first time I had been able to look straight down and see them since my early days with the Yankees.

Now they're being eclipsed again, thanks to those injections.

The important thing in my life at this point is to shake off the pain around my head and fully regain my health. I honestly don't know anybody who wants to live more than I do. It is a driving wish that is always with me these days, a wish that only a person who has been close to death can know and understand.

But it's more than a wish in my case. I've got to stick around a long, long time. For, above everything else, I want to be a part of and help the development of the greatest game God ever saw fit to let man invent—Baseball.

No book about Babe Ruth could be complete without the inclusion of the remarkable statistical records he left in his incomparable wake.

The Big Fellow established or equalled 54 official major league records. Even in cold print they manage to capture, somehow, the enchantment which surrounded all of Ruth's feats. And that's a record in itself.

—BOB CONSIDINE

54 Milestones

Highest slugging percentage, season, 100 or more games—.847—New York, 142 games, 1920 (major league record).

Highest slugging percentage, American League—.692—Boston, New York, 21 years, 1914 to 1934, inclusive (major league record).

Most years leading American League in slugging percentage, 100 or more games—13—Boston, New York, 1918 to 1931, except 1925 (major league record).

Most runs, season (A. L.)—177—New York, 152 games, 1921.

Most years leading American League in runs—8—Boston, New York, 1919, 1920, 1921, 1923, 1924, 1926, 1927, 1928 (major league record).

Most home runs, majors—714—Boston A. L., New York A. L., Boston N. L., 22 years, 1914 to 1935, inclusive. 708 in A. L. and 6 in N. L. *Record now held by Hank Aaron—755 in 21 years*.

Most home runs, American League—708—Boston, New York, 21 years, 1914 to 1934, inclusive. (Hank Aaron hit 733 home runs in the National League).

Most home runs, season—60—New York, 151 games, 1927 (major league record). *Roger Maris hit 61 home runs in 161 games in 1961*.

Most home runs, two consecutive seasons—114—New York, 60 in 1927, 54 in 1928 (major league record).

Most years leading American League in home runs—12—Boston, New York, 1918 (tied), 1919, 1920, 1921, 1923, 1924, 1926, 1927, 1928, 1929, 1930, 1931 (tied) (major league record).

Most consecutive years leading American League in home runs—6—New York, 1926 to 1931 (1931 tied).

Most home runs, season, on road—32—New York, 1927 (major league record).

Most years, 50 or more home runs, American League—4—New York, 1920, 1921, 1927, 1928 (major league record).

Most consecutive years, 50 or more home runs, season, American League—2—New York, 1920-1921; 1927-1928 (major league record).

Most years, 40 or more home runs, American League—11—New York, 1920, 1921, 1923, 1924, 1926, 1927, 1928, 1929, 1930, 1931, 1932 (major league record).

Most consecutive years, 40 or more home runs, American League—7—New York, 1926 to 1932, inclusive (major league record).

Most years, 30 or more home runs, American League—13—New York, 1920 to 1933, excepting 1925.

Most times, two or more home runs, game, in majors—72—Boston A. L., New York A. L., Boston N. L., 22 years, 1914-1935; 71 in American League, 1 in National League.

Most times, two or more home runs, game, American League—71—Boston, New York, 21 years, 1914 to 1934, inclusive.

Most times, three home runs in a double-header—7—New York, 1920 to 1933, inclusive (major league record).

Most home runs, with bases filled, season—4—Boston, 130 games, 1919 (tied A. L. and major league record). *Don Mattingly, in 1987, hit six grandslams in 141 games.*

Most home runs, with bases filled, two consecutive games—2—New York, September 27, 29, 1927, also August 6, second game, August 7, first game, 1929 (tied major league record).

Most home runs, five consecutive games—7—New York, June 10, 11, 12, 13, 14, 1921 (A. L. record and tied major league record). *Since broken by Frank Howard, 1968 (8).*

Most home runs, two consecutive days—6—New York, May 21, 21, 22, 22, 1930, 4 games (tied for major league record).

Most home runs, one week—9—New York, May 18 to 24, second game, 1930, 8 games (tied A. L. record). *Since broken by Frank Howard, 1968 (9).*

Most total bases, season—457, New York, 152 games, 1921 (major league record).

Most years leading American League in total bases—6—Boston, New York, 1919, 1921, 1923, 1924, 1926, 1928 (tied A. L. record).

Most long hits, major leagues—1,358—Boston A. L., New York A. L., Boston N. L., 22 years, 1914 to 1935, inclusive. 506 doubles, 136 triples, 714 home runs. *Record now held by Hank Aaron—1,429 (624 doubles, 98 triples, 755 home runs).*

Most long hits, American League—1,350—Boston, New York, 21 years, 1914 to 1934, inclusive; 506 doubles, 136 triples, 708 home runs.

Most long hits, season—119—New York, 152 games, 1921; 44 doubles, 16 triples, 59 home runs (major league record).

Most years leading American League in long hits—7—Boston, New York, 1918, 1919, 1920, 1921, 1923, 1924, 1928 (tied major league record).

Most consecutive years leading American League in long hits—

4—Boston, New York, 1918, 1919, 1920, 1921 (major league record).

Most extra bases on long hits, in major leagues—2,920—Boston A. L., New York A. L., Boston N. L., 22 years, 1914–1935, inclusive. *Record now held by Hank Aaron—3,085.*

Most extra bases on long hits, American League—2,902—Boston, New York, 21 years, 1914 to 1934, inclusive.

Most extra bases on long hits, season—253—New York, 152 games, 1921 (major league record).

Most years leading American League in extra bases on long hits— 9—Boston, New York, 1918, 1919, 1920, 1921, 1923, 1924, 1926, 1928, 1929 (major league record).

Most consecutive years leading American League in extra bases on long hits—4—Boston, New York, 1918, 1919, 1920, 1921 (major league record).

Most years 200 or more extra bases on long hits—4—New York, 1920, 1921, 1927, 1928 (major league record).

Most years 100 or more extra bases on long hits—14—Boston, New York, 1919 to 1933, inclusive, except 1925 (tied A. L. record). *A. L. record now held by Ted Williams (16).*

Most runs batted in, major leagues—2,209—Boston A. L., New York A. L., Boston N. L., 22 years, 1914 to 1935, inclusive.

Most runs batted in, American League—2,197—Boston, New York, 21 years, 1914 to 1934, inclusive.

Most years leading American League, runs batted in—6—Boston, New York, 1919, 1920, 1921, 1923 (tied), 1926, 1928 (tied).

Most consecutive years leading American League, runs batted in—3—Boston, New York, 1919, 1920, 1921.

Most years, 100 or more runs batted in—13—Boston, New York, 1919 to 1933, except 1922 and 1925 (tied for A. L. and major league record).

Most consecutive years, 150 or more runs batted in, league—3— New York, 1929–30–31 (tied for A. L. and major league record).

Most bases on balls in major leagues—2,056—Boston A. L., New York A. L., Boston N. L., 22 years, 1914 to 1935, inclusive.

Most bases on balls, American League—2,036—Boston, New York, 21 years, 1914 to 1934, inclusive.

Most bases on balls, season—170—New York, 152 games, 1923 (major league record).

Most years leading American League in bases on balls—11—New York, 1920, 1921, 1923, 1924, 1926, 1927, 1928, 1930, 1931, 1932, 1933 (major league record).

Most consecutive years leading American League in bases on balls—4—New York, 1930, 1931, 1932, 1933 (tied for major league record).

Most years 100 or more bases on balls, American League—13—

Boston, New York, 1919, 1920, 1921, 1923, 1924, 1926, 1927, 1928, 1930, 1931, 1932, 1933, 1934 (major league record).

Most consecutive years, 100 or more bases on balls, league—5—New York, 1930 to 1934, inclusive (tied for A. L. record). *A. L. record now held by Edwin Joost—6 (1947–1952).*

Most strikeouts in major leagues—1,330—Boston A. L., New York A. L., Boston N. L., 22 years, 1914 to 1935, inclusive. *Record now held by Reginald Jackson (2,597 in 21 years).*

Most strikeouts, American League—1,306—Boston A. L., New York A.L., 21 years, 1914 to 1934, inclusive. *Record now held by Reginald Jackson (2,597).*

Ruth's Batting and Pitching Records

Year Club	League	G.	AB.	R.	H.	2B.	3B.	HR.	RBI.	B.A.	F.A.
1914– Baltimore-Prov.	Int.	46	121	22	28	2	10	1	..	.231	.964
1914– Boston*	A.L.	5	10	1	2	1	0	0	0	.200	1.000
1915– Boston	A.L.	42	92	16	29	10	1	4	20	.315	.976
1916– Boston	A.L.	67	136	18	37	5	3	3	16	.272	.973
1917– Boston	A.L.	52	123	14	40	6	3	2	10	.325	.984
1918– Boston	A.L.	95	317	50	95	26	11	11	64	.300	.950
1919– Boston†	A.L.	130	432	103	139	34	12	29	112	.322	.990
1920– New York	A.L.	142	458	158	172	36	9	54	137	.376	.936
1921– New York	A.L.	152	540	177	204	44	16	59	170	.378	.966
1922– New York	A.L.	110	403	94	128	24	8	35	96	.315	.964
1923– New York	A.L.	152	522	151	205	45	13	41	130	.393	.973
1924– New York	A.L.	153	529	143	200	39	7	46	121	.378	.962
1925– New York	A.L.	98	359	61	104	12	2	25	66	.290	.974
1926– New York	A.L.	152	495	139	184	30	5	47	155	.372	.979
1927– New York	A.L.	151	540	158	192	29	8	60	164	.356	.963
1928– New York	A.L.	154	536	163	173	29	8	54	142	.323	.975
1929—New York	A.L.	135	499	121	172	26	6	46	154	.345	.984
1930– New York	A.L.	145	518	150	186	28	9	49	153	.359	.965
1931– New York	A.L.	145	534	149	199	31	3	46	163	.373	.972
1932– New York	A.L.	133	457	120	156	13	5	41	137	.341	.961
1933– New York	A.L.	137	459	97	138	21	3	34	103	.301	.970
1934– New York	A.L.	125	365	78	105	17	4	22	84	.288	.962
1935– Boston	N.L.	28	72	13	13	0	0	6	12	.181	.952
Major League Totals ...		2503	8396	2174	2873	506	136	71	2209	.342	.968

*Acquired from Baltimore, July 11, 1914; optioned to Providence, August 20, and recalled at end of International League season, September 27, 1914.

†Sold to New York A.L. for $100,000 and loan of $350,000, January, 1920.

WORLD SERIES RECORDS

Year Club	League	G.	AB.	R.	H.	2B.	3B.	HR.	RBI.	B.A.	F.A.
1915—Boston	A.L.	1	1	0	0	0	0	0	0	.000	.000
1916—Boston	A.L.	1	5	0	0	0	0	0	1	.200	1,000
1918—Boston	A.L.	3	5	0	1	0	1	0	2	.200	1.000
1921—New York	A.L.	6	16	3	5	0	0	1	4	.313	1.000
1922—New York	A.L.	5	17	1	2	1	0	0	1	.118	1.000
1923—New York	A.L.	6	19	8	7	1	1	3	3	.368	.944
1926—New York	A.L.	7	20	6	6	0	0	4	5	.300	1.000
1927—New York	A.L.	4	15	4	6	0	0	2	7	.400	1.000
1928—New York	A.L.	4	16	9	10	3	0	3	3	.625	1.000
1932—New York	A.L.	4	15	6	5	0	0	2	6	.333	.889
World Series Totals		41	129	37	42	5	2	15	32	.325	.977

ALL-STAR GAME RECORD

Year League	AB.	R.	H.	2B.	3B.	HR.	RBI.	B.A.	F.A.
1933—American	4	1	2	0	0	1	2	.500	1.000
1934—American	2	1	0	0	0	0	0	.000	.000
All-Star Game Totals...	6	2	2	0	0	1	2	.333	1.000

PITCHING RECORD

Year Club	League	G.	IP.	W.	L.	Pct.	H.	R.	BB.	SO.	ERA.
1914—Baltimore-Prov	Int.	35	245	22	9	.709	210	88	101	139	...
1914—Boston	A.L.	4	22	2	1	.667	21	12	7	2	3.91
1915—Boston	A.L.	32	218	18	6	.750	166	80	85	112	2.44
1916—Boston	A.L.	44	324	23	12	.657	230	83	118	170	1.75
1917—Boston	A.L.	41	326	23	13	.639	244	93	108	128	2.02
1918—Boston	A.L.	20	166	13	7	.650	125	51	49	40	2.22
1919—Boston	A.L.	17	133	8	5	.615	148	59	58	30	2.97
1920—New York	A.L.	1	4	1	0	1.000	3	4	2	0	4.50
1921—New York	A.L.	2	9	2	0	1.000	14	10	10	2	4.00
1930—New York	A.L.	1	9	1	0	1.000	11	3	3	2	3.00
1933—New York	A.L.	1	9	1	0	1.000	12	5	3	0	5.00
Major League Totals ...		163	1220	92	44	.676	974	400	443	486	2.24

WORLD SERIES PITCHING RECORD

Year Club	League	G.	I.P.	W.	L.	Pct.	H.	R.	BB.	SO.	ERA.
1916—Boston	A.L.	1	14	1	0	1.000	6	1	3	4	0.64
1918—Boston	A.L.	2	17	2	0	1.000	13	2	7	4	1.06
World Series Totals		3	31	3	0	1.000	19	3	10	8	0.87

Courtesy *The Sporting News.*